T0351705

REVISE GCSE
Study Skills GUIDE

Authors: Rob Bircher and Ashley Lodge

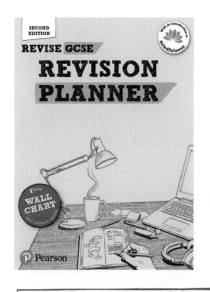

Also available to support your revision:

Revise GCSE Revision Planner
9781292318868

The **Revise GCSE Revision Planner** helps you to plan and organise your time, step-by-step, throughout your GCSE revision. Use this book and wall chart to mastermind your revision.

For the full range of Pearson revision titles across KS2, 11+, KS3, GCSE, Functional Skills, BTEC and AS/A Level visit:

www.pearsonschools.co.uk/revise

Contents

What are study skills?

Study skills are skills you use to improve the way you learn. There are lots of different kinds of study skills. In this book they are grouped into nine separate chapters but, as you'll see, many of them are skills you can use in lots of different situations.

This concept map gives you a very quick introduction to the study skills covered in this book and the area of learning / school life that they cover.

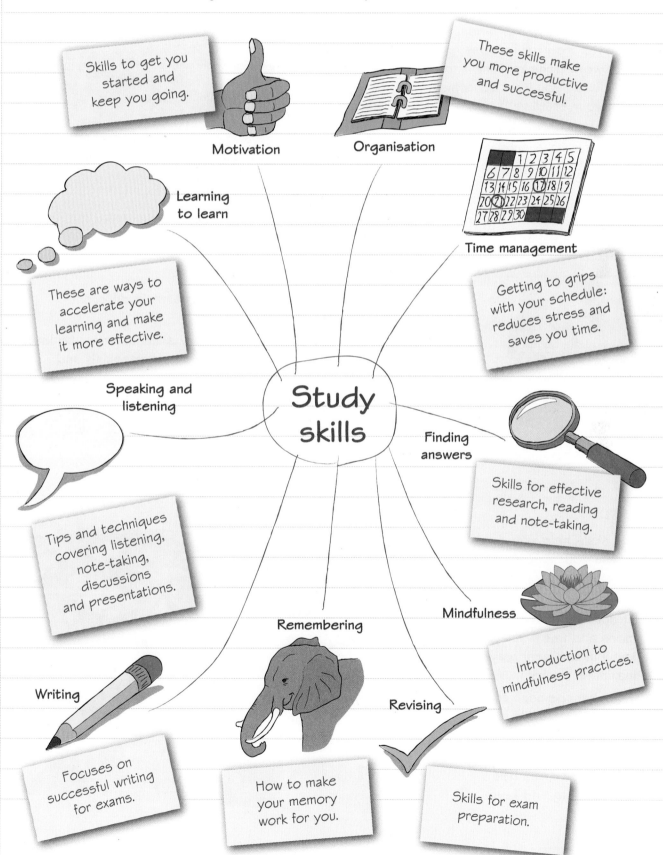

Skills to get you started and keep you going.

Motivation

These skills make you more productive and successful.

Organisation

Learning to learn

Time management

These are ways to accelerate your learning and make it more effective.

Getting to grips with your schedule: reduces stress and saves you time.

Speaking and listening

Study skills

Finding answers

Tips and techniques covering listening, note-taking, discussions and presentations.

Skills for effective research, reading and note-taking.

Mindfulness

Writing

Remembering

Revising

Introduction to mindfulness practices.

Focuses on successful writing for exams.

How to make your memory work for you.

Skills for exam preparation.

Why are study skills important?

Study skills can help you in three main areas at school: managing your life, your different subjects and your exams.

Managing your life

Study skills make school life easier and more enjoyable. How?

- School life is easier when you are prepared for lessons, get your work done on time and know what you want to achieve from your studies.
- School life is more enjoyable when you make sure you have enough time to do the things you want to do.

Different subjects

You may find different study skills important in different subjects. For example:

- For French, you need strong memory skills in order to learn vocabulary and grammar, as well as good speaking and listening skills.
- For Science, you need analysis and problem-solving skills.
- For English or Business Studies, you need to be able to evaluate and write fluently using well-constructed text.

Exams

Study skills help you do better in your exams. How?

- Revision skills and memory skills help you revise effectively, remember more and use what you know in the best ways to maximise marks.
- Time management and organisation skills help you spend enough time revising all your subjects.
- Motivation skills get you revising and keep you going.

How study skills are linked to job skills

Learning study skills is essential if you want to do well – not just in your school work and in your exams, but for your future after school too. Look for the skills these three job adverts are asking for.

Jobs - 4 - You

Home   Next   Prev

Full time legal secretary

Must have good communication, organisational and IT skills.

Previous experience in an office environment an advantage.

Applications in writing with a CV to:

Saskia DeVine, DeVine Solicitors, 29 Legal Street, Erewhon ER1 123

You will learn about communication skills in Chapter 5 and Chapter 7.

This would link with skills from Chapters 2 and 3 – organisation and time management are closely related.

CV stands for curriculum vitae: it is a summary of your achievements, skills, experience and interests.

JobApplications.com

Retail opportunities at new superstore

Have you got what it takes to be part of our award-winning superstore team?

- Are you a self-starter who gets the job done?
- Do you enjoy learning new skills?
- Do you have great teamwork skills and a positive attitude?

Retail experience is not essential: we provide all training and you'll earn a qualification, too.

Call 0394 881 9034 for an appointment at our local open day.

‹‹‹   ›››

Employers are often looking for people who can motivate themselves, rather than having to be told what to do all the time. Chapter 1 has tips about motivation.

Learning is something you'll do your whole life – it is not just for school. Chapter 4 is all about learning how to learn.

Some of the study skills in this book are just for you, but many are about working with others too.

Last   Next

Magazine work experience

An amazing opportunity to develop design, editorial, marketing and sales skills and experience in Erewhon's vibrant city centre.

Successful candidates will be creative individuals with excellent time management skills. We are looking for confident communicators with big career aspirations.

Please apply in writing by sending your CV and a covering letter that really showcases your creative side to:

workexp@erewhonmagz.com

Study skills can help you think creatively. You can learn more about this in Chapter 4.

The time management skills you learn for school are directly transferable to every other part of your life – see Chapter 3 for more.

Study skills can cover all sorts of communication, including how to present information effectively, as demonstrated in Chapters 5 and 7.

Now try this

Write a job advert for a good GCSE student. What skills would they need to do well in their course and get good grades in their final exams? Look through this book to give yourself some ideas.

3

Layers of learning

Experts have found that there are different layers to learning – there is more to it than many people realise. Study skills are one important way to get access to deeper layers of learning.

① Surface learning

Surface learning is about learning the building blocks of knowledge – often factual information.

For example, understanding and learning vocabulary in languages, equations in Physics, or the names of components of a cell in Biology.

Study skills help surface learning by:

- helping you to find effective ways to learn facts
- helping you to memorise the facts for a test
- giving you methods to build your surface learning through making connections with other facts.

Surface learning is a crucial starting point – once you have learned the facts, you can move onto applying your knowledge.

Techniques such as mnemonics and weird pairs can help you with surface learning.

② Deep learning

Deep learning is about applying your knowledge to a situation, or making connections between facts. For example, identifying the formulae required to solve a Maths problem and then using those in the right order, applied to that specific problem.

Study skills help deep learning because:

- techniques such as SQ3R can help develop deep learning by helping you connect and apply facts
- if you are interested in improving your study skills, you are already on your way to deep learning.

Deep learning is great for creative, high-quality work and learning that you will remember more easily.

③ Strategic learning

Strategic learning happens when you understand why you need to know facts, and when surface approaches and deep approaches are required.

It is when you learn what you need to do well.

It's called strategic learning because it's learning with a plan.

Study skills help strategic learning by:

- helping you manage your time effectively
- boosting your motivation to stay on track
- showing you how to get the most out of your lessons
- improving your learning with memory techniques and insights into exams.

Some subjects may have hidden treasures for you that only deep learning can uncover.

How this book works

This book has been designed so you can use it in different ways, depending on what you are looking for.

1 Top tips

Procrastination solved

If you are looking for a particular solution to a study problem (strategic learning), then top tips are a good place to start.

Each chapter starts with a page that outlines what the chapter contains, including objectives. Top tips are listed here. They aim to provide you with a ready-made technique that you can get going with very quickly.

This book is underpinned by research into study skills and what can work for students like you. Look out for **It's true!** icons which indicate specific instances where techniques have helped others in similar situations.

Terms in red are explained in the glossary. **Page 98**

2 Try it out and Now try this

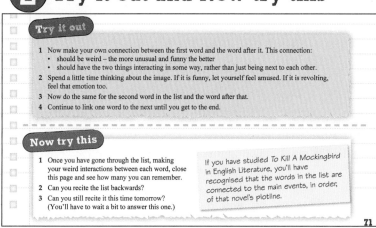

Try it out

1 Now make your own connection between the first word and the word after it. This connection:
   • should be weird – the more unusual and funny the better
   • should have the two things interacting in some way, rather than just being next to each other.
2 Spend a little time thinking about the image. If it is funny, let yourself feel amused. If it is revolting, feel that emotion too.
3 Now do the same for the second word in the list and the word after that.
4 Continue to link one word to the next until you get to the end.

Now try this

1 Once you have gone through the list, making your weird interactions between each word, close this page and see how many you can remember.
2 Can you recite the list backwards?
3 Can you still recite it this time tomorrow? (You'll have to wait a bit to answer this one.)

If you have studied To Kill A Mockingbird in English Literature, you'll have recognised that the words in the list are connected to the main events, in order, of that novel's plotline.

71

Each page gives you information about a study skill or skills, and there will often be an opportunity or opportunities to try out that skill for yourself.

Trying a study skill out for yourself means you can evaluate it – decide if it is any good to you.

Once you know which skills work for you (maybe after a bit of tweaking), you can put them into action when you need them.

3 Challenges

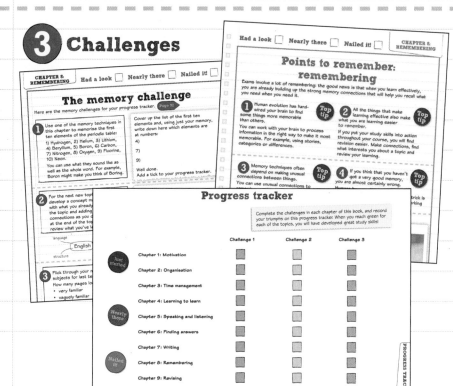

At the end of each chapter are four points to remember – reflection points about the chapter.

Each chapter also has a challenge just before the points to remember.

There are three levels to complete, and each level takes your learning deeper.

The challenges should help motivate your learning.

Setting goals is a very important part of really effective learning.

Completing the challenges in this book could be one goal you'd like to set yourself. Good luck!

Getting ready for study

There are all sorts of different ways to learn and what works for one person doesn't always work for everyone.

If you can treat your studying like a martial art – something that needs focus, skill and discipline – then these could be the rules for your study dojo.

If that sounds over the top, then here are a few tips that will always get your studying off to a good start.

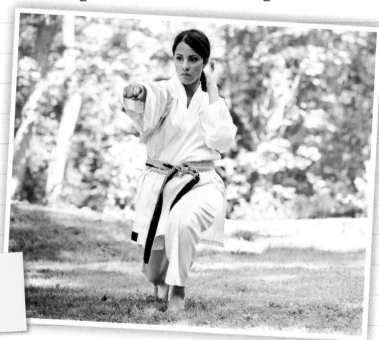

Your study dojo is a state of mind – you can take it anywhere!

Your study dojo

Before you enter the study dojo

- Your brain needs a minimum of eight hours' sleep every night to perform at its best.
- A healthy breakfast will give you energy all morning for study.
- Studying at the same time each day builds a routine, making it easier to get started.

When you enter the study dojo

- Make sure you have everything you need. Switch off any distractions. If you focus on your work you will get it done quicker and better than if you are distracted.
- Begin your study session with five minutes of warm-up exercise. Do star jumps or run on the spot, stretch your limbs, do a dance. This will give you energy.
- Then sit calmly for one minute, focusing on your breathing. This will clear your mind and get it ready for action.

During your study session

- Do not attempt too much study at once. Start with fifteen minutes of study, then a five-minute break, then another fifteen minutes.

Ending your study session

- Sit for one minute, thinking through what you have learned. This kind of reflection is a key technique for deep learning.

If this all sounds good but you're not sure you've got the motivation to see it through, Chapter 1 should help – it's all about motivation.

Study skills and motivation

You are more likely to want to do something if you can see the point of it and understand why it is relevant to you. So what might motivate you to learn some study skills?

Motivation

Motivation is about how much you want to do something. Good study skills boost your confidence at school because they:

- help you learn effectively – so you get more from what you do
- help you manage your learning – so you feel more in control of all the things you have to do.

Study skills helped us get better GCSE grades because we learned about effective revision and how to prepare for exams.

Learning good ways to find information that I can trust has been so useful. And I find my study skills also help me remember key information.

Learning about study skills made me more confident about school and more motivated generally.

Objectives

Your learning objectives in this chapter

Techniques that give your motivation levels a boost

- Procrastination and how to beat it.   Page 8
- How chunking makes big projects doable.   Page 9
- Using rewards to increase motivation.   Page 10

How setting goals can power up long-term motivation

- Thinking ahead and setting a goal.   Page 11
- Understanding the difference between goals and objectives.   Page 12

Study skills and your future

- The motivation challenge.   Page 13
- Points to remember.   Page 14

It's true!

Research has shown that if you are really motivated, you can achieve more than others who might be more intelligent but less motivated. The key to being motivated is finding out why your studies matter to you and how to get the confidence to succeed.

It has also been shown that confidence in your own ability to learn promotes success. Students who use study skills effectively are more likely to believe that they can learn. Therefore, they are more likely to be successful.

Now try this

1 Which page(s) of this chapter could help with getting started with a task – a task you keep putting off and putting off, for example?

2 Which page(s) of this chapter could help convince someone that study skills are worth learning about?

Procrastination

It can sometimes be really hard to get going with a project. Procrastination means using distractions to avoid doing something. It is a big drain on motivation, but this page provides a procrastinator-breaker.

Know your enemy

It's good to relax and have a break from work, and some tasks are a lot easier if you have a think about how you are going to achieve them first.

But procrastination is a problem when it makes you start to feel annoyed or frustrated or guilty about your work, or when it causes stress between you and others.

Luckily, there's a really easy solution to solving any problematic procrastination!

'The best way to do it, is to do it.'
Amelia Earhart, pioneer aviator

'If you hear a voice within you say "you cannot paint", then by all means paint, and that voice will be silenced.'
Vincent van Gogh

Sometimes we put off doing something because we worry we won't be able to achieve it. Many inspirational people say they succeeded simply because they just got on with it.

Procrastination solved

◉◉◐◯◯ SupaTel
Countdown
0:01:57
Play tune when countdown ends
Start   Stop

Top tip

All you need to do to beat procrastination is to do just two minutes of the task you are putting off.

That's all – just two minutes. You can use an egg timer or a stopwatch if you like.

Why does it work?

The reason why the two-minute rule often helps beat procrastination is that your brain hates incomplete tasks.

So once you start something for two minutes, you'll often find yourself happily continuing with it till it's done.

Now try this

Think of a job you've been putting off doing for a while.

Perhaps sorting out a folder of notes from school? Page 16

Or putting together a revision planner? Page 80

Try out the 'procrastinator solved' procrastinator-breaker technique on it. Did getting started on a job help you to keep going with it? If not, read the next page, and see if chunking the task could make a difference.

Ways to get motivated

Do you ever look at a task and think: 'There's just too much to do. I don't even know how to get started'? One simple way to make a task easier is to break it into chunks.

How to chunk

Top tip

The best way to get through big or complex tasks or projects is to:

- break them down into manageable chunks
- write down what might make each chunk difficult to achieve (problems / challenges you might face)
- decide what your reward for achieving each chunk will be.

Make sure each chunk is manageable. If they are too big or hard to achieve, chunking won't work that well.

One really motivating way to achieve a project is to tell other people about it. That makes it real.

Weirdly, identifying the ways in which things can go wrong usually helps to get things done.

It's true!

Research shows that people who just daydream about projects tend not to cope so well when things don't go to plan.

Three keys to motivation

Three things really help to make something motivating.

1 If something is interesting and / or fun.

2 If something is important – it matters.

3 If you get to do something your way.

Breaking complex tasks up into manageable chunks is an important technique for many study skills, including exam revision. It's also the starting point for planning your time.

It's true!

Even if people are paid good money to do a job, studies show that they are less motivated than people who get to work out for themselves how best to do the same job – often unpaid!

Here are some ideas for ways to make study tasks more interesting.

- Set time challenges to get through each section of the task.
- Go and tell someone about what you have to do. You will often find that this makes deciding what you need to do much clearer.
- Find someone to work on the task with you.
- Pack up your stuff and take your study task somewhere different.
- Link what you are doing to something important that you hope to achieve.

Linking tasks to something important is connected to setting goals. Page 12

Now try this

Design a simple routine to help you stay healthy during your exams. The regime needs to include diet, exercise, relaxation and sleep. It should include some ways to keep yourself motivated. How could the tips on this page help you with this task?

Games and rewards

Video game developers are experts in motivation. Often a lot of what you have to do in a game can be quite boring and repetitive. But in really good games, the designers build in lots of little rewards to keep players motivated.

Rewards

Game designers get players to do things in a game by giving out rewards, such as:

- finding information – moving on the story
- more gold / credits
- earning skills points / skills upgrade
- new weapons / mods (modifications)
- 'Easter eggs' – hidden items to collect.

> Understanding how games use rewards to motivate players could help you design rewards to help you achieve your objectives.

Upgrade your skills

In many games, characters earn upgrades by developing different skills and powers.
For example:

- Search Engine – uncover hidden knowledge
- Empath – understand the thoughts of others
- Words of Power – persuade others to agree with you
- Mighty Mind – solve puzzles
- Master / Mistress of Time – bend time to accomplish tasks easily
- Cook Up a Storm – create power-ups using everyday ingredients
- Summoner – recall and unleash words of power when it really matters.

Try it out

1 Imagine you are the game designer responsible for working out how to motivate players to complete these character upgrades. Use a table like the one below to decide:

(a) what tasks characters would need to complete to develop their skills

(b) how you would reward the character for completing each task or chunk of tasks.

Powers	Tasks	Rewards
Search Engine		
Empath		
Words of Power		
Mighty Mind		
Master / Mistress of Time		
Cook Up a Storm		
Summoner		

Now try this

1 Can you work out which study skills each of these powers relates to?

2 Now think of some real-life rewards you could use to motivate your studies – be creative but practical.

Motivation and setting goals

Getting tasks underway, breaking complex tasks into manageable chunks and giving yourself rewards are good tips to get a motivation boost. A longer-lasting technique is to set goals for yourself and link tasks to those goals. This works because you are more motivated to do things when you can see why they are important.

Setting goals

Job interviews often include this question:
'Where do you see yourself in two years' time?'

We can use this kind of question to help set goals for study, too.

Where do you see yourself in two years' time?

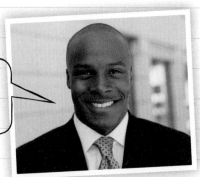

Where I see myself in two years' time

Use this space to write your answer. Make it as detailed as you can. What do you want to be doing in two years' time?

....
....
....
....
....
....
....
....
....
....
....
....
....
....
....
....

How does study fit in?

What qualifications do you think you will need to achieve this goal?

....
....
....
....

What skills might you need to develop to achieve this goal?

....
....
....
....

Anything else you will need from your school studies?

....
....
....

Now try this

Where you see yourself in two years' time is an example of a personal goal. Copy out your answer and pin it up so you can see it when you study at home. If you can link your study tasks to steps on the way to achieving your goal, that should help you feel motivated to do them.

Goals and objectives

Objectives are steps on the way to achieving a goal. Read these two scenarios and decide which bits are describing goals and which bits are describing objectives.

Kai:

'I want to study Psychology at university because I'm really interested in what makes people behave the way they do. I'm doing GCSE Psychology already but I need to get good grades in English and Maths too to take it further, and I'll need a really good grade in a science subject at A Level, plus two good grades in another two A Levels.'

Kai's goal is to:

....

....

Kai's objectives to achieve this goal are:

....

....

....

Louis:

'I really want to get a job in social media, perhaps in user support because I already help lots of my friends with user issues. I need to build up my teamwork skills, do research into job requirements and I've heard it would really help if I did some volunteer work in a customer support role, like an online moderator.'

Louis's goal is to:

....

....

Louis's objectives to achieve this goal are:

....

....

....

Now try this

Use this shape to record three objectives towards your 'me in two years' time' goals.

Goal:

Objective 3:

Objective 2:

Objective 1:

The motivation challenge

Your study skills goal is up to you but, if you like, completing the progress tracker could be another objective to help you on your way to your main goal. Page 97

To earn it, you need to complete three tasks for each of the nine study skill challenges – one for each chapter. This is the motivation challenge.

1 Next time you keep putting something off, use the procrastinator-breaker technique to get the job started.

Use this space to describe how you completed the challenge.

Well done.
Add a tick to your progress tracker. ●

2 Decide what your three top study rewards are going to be – ways to motivate yourself to finish a study task – and complete three tasks to check they work.

Use this space to list your three rewards and the three tasks you completed to trial them.

1

2

3

Well done.
Add a tick to your progress tracker. ●

3

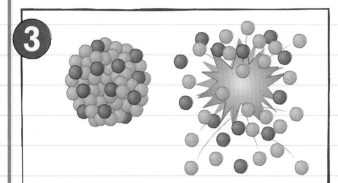

Pick one subject you do that you find difficult. Set yourself three objectives that will help you towards a rewarding goal with this subject.

Name of subject:

Your goal for this subject:

Your three objectives:
1

2

3

Well done.
Add a tick to your progress tracker. ●

Quick quiz

1 Which page in this chapter includes Easter eggs?
2 Who said 'The best way to do it, is to do it'?

Points to remember: motivation

You can learn to motivate yourself to take on challenges. It is a very important skill to have and one that will help you all through your studies and in your life afterwards.

1 Remember that your brain hates to leave things unfinished.

If you decide to just do something for two minutes, it's more than likely you will get into it and even enjoy getting the job done.

2 Writing down the problems you think you might encounter during a task actually helps your motivation.

It's people who don't anticipate problems who often face big motivation challenges.

3 Splitting a big task into chunks works well, especially if you build in some little rewards for getting each chunk done.

If you want to learn about motivation and rewards the fun way, study how video games are designed.

4 The most powerful motivation comes from setting yourself real goals.

This is because if you can see how a task helps you reach your goal, then completing that task becomes important and relevant to you.

Motivational quotes

These quotes by famous people may help inspire and motivate you:

'The most certain way to succeed is always to try just one more time.'
Thomas Edison, inventor

'Whether you think you can or you think you can't, you're right.'
Henry Ford, industrial pioneer

'The best time to plant a tree was 20 years ago. The second best time is now.'
Chinese proverb

'Whatever you can do, or dream you can, begin it. Boldness has genius, power and magic in it.'
Johann Wolfgang von Goethe, writer and politician

'Start where you are. Use what you have. Do what you can.'
Arthur Ashe, tennis champion

'How wonderful it is that nobody need wait a single moment before starting to improve the world.'
Anne Frank, famous diarist

Now try this

1 Read the quotes on motivation. Decide which one is your favourite and explain why.
2 What would your advice be to someone who wanted to know how to get more motivated to study?

Organisational skills

Being a bit more organised with your studies can improve how well you do your work, how long it takes you to complete tasks and how you feel about your studies.

Objectives

Your objectives are about how to organise your stuff so you can:
- find what you need when you need it **Page 16**
- get the most out of your planner. **Page 17**

'To do' lists can:
- help prioritise and set times for tasks **Page 18**
- be accessed from online list management tools. **Page 19**

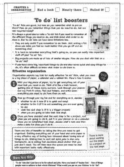

You can super-charge your 'to do' lists to get more done and feel less stressed. **Page 20**

Planning ahead involves thinking about the steps involved in completing a project. **Page 21**

It's true!

Researchers recently found that students who improve their organisation skills achieve better academically, have fewer homework problems and argue less with their families.

Getting organised

Lots of students find getting organised for school quite difficult.
- They might be used to someone organising things for them (e.g. parents, their teachers).
- They're so busy with other activities that it feels like there's no time to organise.

The good news is that there are lots of tips to help you get a bit more organised, in both this chapter and the next.

Now try this

1 A student regularly forgets to bring their homework back to school. Which page of this chapter could help them solve this organisational problem?

2 A student often forgets that there's a test coming up and isn't prepared. Which page would help them get this issue under control?

Finding what you need

If you can find what you need when you need it, then you can get tasks done more quickly and efficiently. This will save you time and effort.

Keep what you need

Go through all your study stuff and get rid of anything you don't need. This makes it easier to find what you do need.

Organise your work

Get a folder and some dividers. You need a divider for each subject / class. Always put all your notes and handouts into their proper section. Everything needs a home.

Sort out your bag

Empty your bag at the end of each day. Dump the stuff you don't need. Sort everything you do need into its proper home. Pack your bag with what you need for the next day.

Study area

Sort out a study area at home. Make sure this has the things you need right there so you don't have to hunt for them – phone charger, pens, paper, stapler, hole punch, calculator, dictionary.

Organise your computer

If you use a computer or tablet at home, organise your files and folders the same way they are organised at school or college.

Bookmarks

Organise your computer's bookmarks into your subject areas to keep track of useful websites.

Or use a productivity tool such as Microsoft Edge, Evernote or Diigo to store, organise and add notes to useful websites. That way you'll be able to find them again when you need them.

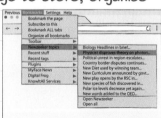

Now try this

If you spend time getting everything sorted instead of doing your work, then that can be **counterproductive**. So spend ten minutes now planning what you need to do to get sorted, then for the next few days spend ten minutes a day putting your plan into action.

Making the most of your planner

Your school planner is your paper-based best friend. Here are some tips on getting maximum benefit from what your planner has to offer.

Using a planner

To get the most out of your planner or homework diary / journal, you need to be organised about how you use it. Here are some tips to maximise your full planner potential.

When you are writing down homework assignments, make sure you record when the homework has to be done by.

Make a note if your teacher has given you any handouts to use in your homework.

If you are allowed to, take a photo of the instructions about the homework on the board. Note in your planner that you've got a picture – just put 'pic' or something quick.

Colour coding

Top tip

Colour code different kinds of notes using highlighters. This will help you see what you've got on more easily.

For example: green for social events, yellow for homework, blue for personal reminders, pink with CAPITAL LETTERS for DEADLINES DUE THIS WEEK!

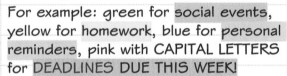

Try to write clearly too, so you don't have any problems deciphering your scribbles.

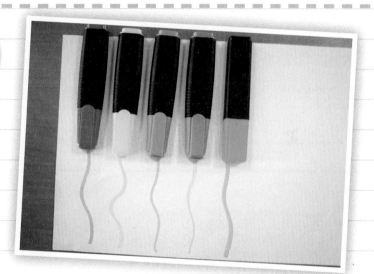

'To do' lists

Incorporate a 'to do' list for each week in your planner.

Make this a smart 'to do' list by leaving space to write in what things you need to have in order to get each item done.

For example, if you need to call someone whose number isn't in your phone, write their number down next to that item on your list.

Many of the items on your list will be part of the objectives you have put together to help you reach your goals.

Try it out

Use your planner to plan!

- As well as just writing down what your teacher tells you to write down, think ahead.
- Identify days when you are going to be really busy and plan how to fit everything in.
- Get the dates of tests and exams into your planner so you can start to prepare for them in time. It is never too early to plan for these.
- Try to schedule assignments so you can finish them early – that is a very impressive study skill. It also frees you up for other things you enjoy doing.

Now try this

Compare the way you use your planner with other students. What can you learn from them about how to make your planner work better for you? Put your findings into practice.

'To do' lists

Rather than keeping everything you need to do in your head, it makes a lot of sense to write it down in a 'to do' list. Then you can start to plan how you are going to tackle it.

A 'to do' list is a list of things you need to do.

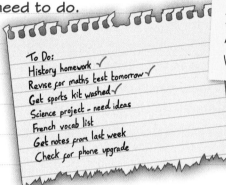

To Do:
History homework ✓
Revise for maths test tomorrow ✓
Get sports kit washed ✓
Science project - need ideas
French vocab list
Get notes from last week
Check for phone upgrade

A 'to do' list is a great way of keeping track of what you need to do.
All you do is make a list of what you have to do today.
When you've done something, you tick it off.

Writing down what you have to do means your mind doesn't have to spend so much time and effort trying to remember it all.

Prioritising

To take your 'to do' list to the next level, prioritise the most important things.

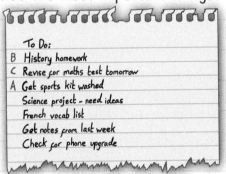

To Do:
B History homework
C Revise for maths test tomorrow
A Get sports kit washed
   Science project - need ideas
   French vocab list
   Get notes from last week
   Check for phone upgrade

Top tip

Many people pick the top three things on the list – the absolutely most vital things – and order them A, B and C. Then do them in that order.

Most things in life take about twice as long to do as we think they will. Prioritising items on a list is very important.

Time targets

A really high level 'to do' list not only has priorities but time targets too.

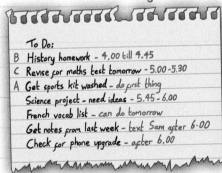

To Do:
B History homework - 4.00 till 4.45
C Revise for maths test tomorrow - 5.00-5.30
A Get sports kit washed - do first thing
   Science project - need ideas - 5.45-6.00
   French vocab list - can do tomorrow
   Get notes from last week - text Sam after 6.00
   Check for phone upgrade - after 6.00

Adding time targets for when you aim to finish each task can be a really motivational way to power through a list.
Don't set yourself impossible targets though, or you'll struggle. Build in a bit more time than you think you'll need.

Top tip

If your 'to do' list is going to take a lot of time, try to plan in a break. A break is a good reward, which helps with your motivation.

Now try this

1 Write out a 'to do' list for what you want to get done tomorrow.
2 Which are the three most important things? Prioritise them using A, B and C.
3 Try out time targets as a way of working through a list. Is it motivational for you, or not?

Examiners' report

"Higher-scoring answers often have plans."

Make sure you remain organised in the exam – it is usually best to plan your answers for longer essay questions.

Help with lists

If you find that you keep losing your 'to do' lists, or you find that it doesn't suit you to keep them in your planner, then there are lots of different online tools that will keep your lists in one place. If these tools help you to stay on top of what you need to do, then they can be worthwhile.

> There are so many great ways to record and organise your 'to do' lists that it can be hard to know where to start.
>
> The danger can be that each one promises to make you better organised, so you keep trying different ones.
>
> That is a bit like spending time making lists look pretty. Your lists should be helping you to take action, not wasting your time.

List managers

Only you can choose the best way to manage your 'to do' lists, but take a look at these five popular apps / websites that have been around for a while.

Google Tasks (part of Gmail)

Remember the Milk

Microsoft To Do

Popular list managers

Todoist

Evernote

Stick with free options. You can get organised enough without spending money on productivity apps or upgrades. Remember, too, that using paper and pen can be quicker than an app and just as effective.

Top tip

What you want from your list system

- One that is always with you – so you can add to lists whenever you need to.
- Syncs across platforms – nothing does this better than paper and pen!
- Quick and easy to use.
- Helps you prioritise your list.
- Adds 'to-dos' to your calendar / planner.
- Lets you sort lists into different subjects – great for study.

What you *don't* want from your list system

- A different system on each device – one on your phone, one on your tablet plus six lists on scraps of paper scattered round your house.
- Something you can't access when you are at school or college, e.g. if phones aren't allowed in lessons.
- Too complex for what you need it to do.
- Takes too long to upload / open.

Now try this

Find your perfect 'to do' list manager. Try out a few options and see which one works best for you.

'To do' list boosters

'To do' lists are good, but how do you remember what to put on them? How do you remember things that you do need to do, but are not required today?

It's always a good idea to make a 'to do' list if you need to remember all the different things you need to do, and think about what order to do them in. But 'to do' lists can have some limitations too.

- They are only useful if you remember to do them. Just writing a list down can make you feel so much better that you go off and do something else!

- It is hard to remember everything that's going on, so you can easily miss important stuff off your 'to do' list.

- Big projects are made up of lots of smaller stages. How do you deal with that on a 'to do' list?

- If you have some big, important things to do and also some quick and easy things to do, it's often difficult to know what order to do them in.

Effective organisation

Top tip

Organisation experts say that, for really effective 'to do' lists, what you need is a big piece of paper, a calendar and a rubbish bin. Here's how it works:

1 With your big piece of paper, try to get everything out of your mind that you need to do. Think of it like a brain hoover, getting into all those dusty corners. Look through your planner and any Post-It notes, files and folders, and write down everything you need to do from them as well.

2 Now go through your big list and for everything on it, decide:
- whether to do it now (if it is quick and easy)
- whether to bin it (if it is not something you will do)
- what the next step is (if it is a bigger project)
- when you are going to take that next step.

3 Once you have decided the next step, and when you are going to do it, put it in your planner or on a calendar. Then decide what's next and then make a date for when you'll do it.

There are lots of benefits to taking the time you need to get organised. Getting everything out of your head and onto paper is an effective way of feeling less stressed about having lots of things to do. Making time to sort out quick jobs is also very therapeutic, as is making final decisions about clutter. You will then have the space you need to deal with important tasks really effectively.

There is more about working out the steps to a project on the next page.

There is more about working out the steps to a project on the next page.

Now try this

'To do' lists don't just have to be for school and jobs. Have you heard of 'bucket lists' – lists of things people want to achieve in their whole lifetimes? What would you put on your lifetime 'to do' list?

Planning ahead

A 'to do' list is a good way of making sure you complete different tasks and prioritising which tasks are most important. The next step in organisation is planning. Planning involves really taking control of a project and deciding how best to complete it.

Working out the steps

A plan is the process of working out the steps (objectives) you need to take to make a project come together successfully to achieve a goal.

Getting the plan together

Use Post-It notes to work out everything that needs to happen for you to achieve your goal.

You can move the notes around until you've got them in the order you think will work best.

For example, Evie and Reuben want to make an online video on study skills for an end-of-term assignment. Here are their Post-It notes:

Borrow Adel's phone (HD video).

Film in R's room.

E to present. Bring planner.

Use iMovie for edit (on dad's Mac).

Need microphone.

Clear up R's room.

Bring highlighter pens.

What about music?

Check if we can use YouTube in school.

Schedules and deadlines

Once you have worked out the steps in your plan you should decide:

- what resources you need
- who is going to do each step (if there's more than one person involved)
- how long each step is going to take (this is usually the most difficult part to get right!).

Then you can write out a schedule for your plan: what dates each step should be achieved by and the final deadline.

The biggest planning operation in your GCSE course will probably be planning your revision. You can find out more about how to do this in Chapter 9.

Revising for different subjects all at the same time needs effective planning.

Your teachers will help you organise yourself so you have a schedule to work to and the resources you need for your studies.

Now try this

A GCSE Design and Technology student has been given an assignment to design a shopping bag for sale at the Eden Project in Cornwall. The bag should be made from recycled materials and the design should reflect the values and branding of the Eden Project. The student has four weeks to complete their design and a presentation that explains how it fits the project brief. Outline a plan for completing this project: steps, order of steps, resources, schedule and deadline.

The organisation challenge

Remember your progress tracker? Here are your tasks for the organisation challenge.

Page 97

1 Write a 'to do' list at the start of a week on a page in your planner. If you have ticked off more than 50 per cent of the things on your list by the end of the week, you have succeeded.

Week ___ with ___ weeks to go

Day	Session A	Session B	Session C	Session D	Session E	Rewards
Monday						
Tuesday						
Wednesday						
Thursday						

91

Write in the percentage of things you ticked off your week's 'to do' list here:

(To calculate your percentage, divide the number of things you ticked off by the total number of things on your list and multiply by 100.)
Well done.
Add a tick to your progress tracker. ●

2

Empty your bag at the end of each day. Dump the stuff you don't need. Sort everything you do need into its proper home. Pack your bag with what you need for the next day. Do this every night for five school nights.

Use this space to evaluate this organisation method: say what was good about it and what things did not work so well.

Well done.
Add a tick to your progress tracker. ●

3

- Organise your school folder or folders so you have all your notes for each subject in one place.
- Organise your notes so information on each topic is all kept together. You could use a colour-coding system for this.
- Check your notes against the notes and handouts for each topic you've done so far that are stored on your school VLE or network. Make sure you get copies of any notes you have missed.

Make a note here of all the subjects you have organised your notes for and any that have notes missing that you need to amend. If you haven't yet organised the notes for all your subjects, put a date when you will do this by, and a reward to motivate yourself!

Well done.
Add a tick to your progress tracker. ●

Quick quiz

1 What page in this chapter mentions washing your sports kit?
2 How does your brain hate to leave things?

Points to remember: organisation

Organisation is a skill everyone can learn and it puts you in control of what you do and how you do it.

1 Being organised means you can get tasks done more quickly and efficiently. This will save you time and effort.

Sorting everything out takes a while to begin with, but you'll soon get that time back from being more organised.

Top tip

2 Making good use of your planner puts you in control of your learning. Make sure you always have it with you and keep it up to date.

That way, you will know what needs to be done and when it needs to be done by. You can prioritise your tasks and be ready for tests and exams.

Top tip

3 Use lists to keep track of what you need to do. Lists help you prioritise your tasks and feel motivated as you tick each one off.

Trying to remember a long list of things gets exhausting. Let a list take the strain.

Top tip

4 Planning your revision or a big project is essential because there are different steps that need to happen in the right order.

Planning ahead means you can avoid a lot of the stress of completing an important project and ensure you don't run out of time.

Top tip

School report

Read this section from a school report then answer the question at the bottom of the page.

Oliver frequently forgets to do his homework, or he leaves it at home and hands it in late. He did not do as well as he should on the end-of-term test because he could not find notes for some of this term's lessons.

I know he has tried to use a range of different apps to keep track of things on his phone, but every week he seems to be using something new! He stuffs handouts into his bag rather than putting them in a folder, and his planner is a mess: full of loose bits of paper and doodles.

He is not prepared for tests – they seem to be a complete surprise to him, even though his teachers give him plenty of warning.

Oliver is a bright student who could do much better with just a little more organisation of his studies.

S. Watson

Mrs Sarah Watson
Head of Year

Now try this

Using what you know about organisational skills, highlight different problems raised in Oliver's report and suggest ways in which he could tackle each one.

Why is time management important?

Time management is key to being organised. What can good time management do for you?

Now I plan my time more carefully I am much more in control of my life. I feel a *lot* less stressed.

Using my study time more effectively has been great. I'm more prepared and my teachers say my work has really improved.

It's essential that all my students are here at the start of each lesson because that's when I explain what the lesson is all about.

What I like most about time management skills is that they actually save you time to do the things you like the most.

Examiners' report

"*The use of corrective fluid (e.g. Tipp-Ex or Liquid Paper) is strictly not allowed.*"
Don't use corrective fluid in the exam – it is not allowed and wastes time. Just cross out any mistakes you make in the exam as neatly as you can.

It's true!

Research has shown that the better a student manages their time, the better their grades and the less stress they experience in their academic life generally.

Objectives

Your learning objectives in this chapter

- Discovering tools and tips for getting to grips with time.   Pages 25 and 26
- Working out the best times for study in your week.   Pages 27 and 28
- Protecting your time and using it productively.   Pages 29 and 30

Now try this

1 Which page(s) of this chapter help you to plan when you are going to study?
2 Which page(s) of this chapter help you to protect your time by saying 'no'?

Time management tools

One key to using your time effectively is to have a good view of what's coming up. You can use different tools to get a different focus on your time.

'**To do**' lists organise the time you have available each day.

- Use them to prioritise what you need to do.
- You can also work out how much time to give to each task on your list.

Find out more on using 'to do' lists.

Pages 18 and 19

Planners give you a view of what's happening week by week.

- Plan ahead so you are well prepared for each day.
- Write down when work is due so you can hand it in on time.
- Use your lesson timetable so you are on time for the start of all lessons.

Find out more about planners.

Page 17

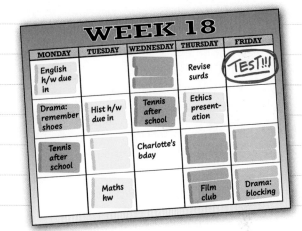

A **calendar** shows a month at a time. You may have a family calendar at home. Check this for things you are doing as a family when you are updating your planner.

A **yearly planner** shows the whole year in one go. You can use one of these to look a long way ahead and keep track of where you are in relation to big events such as exams and holidays, school trips, concerts, etc.

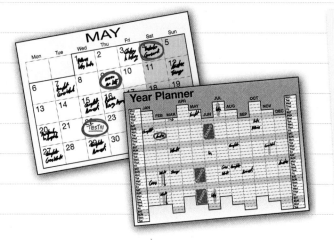

Now try this

Calendar apps can switch between different views (daily, weekly, monthly), and remind you of what you need to do. What are the pros and cons of using a calendar app and using a paper planner? How could you use them together for really advanced time management?

Time management tips

These tips will help you get control over your time so you can make the most of it.

Planner tips

You need to be able to depend on your planner to tell you what's coming up.

- Always keep your planner with you.
- Take care: it's easy to write things on the wrong day by mistake.
- You can use abbreviations to save time: write a T for test, NH for no homework, etc. Always use the same ones so you don't forget what they mean.
- For each deadline / test you put in your planner, decide when you are going to do the work involved and put that in your planner too.
- Review your planner at the start and end of each day. Carry forward things you have not achieved.

Getting up

- Make sure you get plenty of rest – by going to bed earlier rather than sleeping in late!
- If you use your phone alarm or alarm clock, put it the other side of the room from your bed – that way you'll have to get up to switch it off.
- Have everything ready the night before so you can save time in the morning.

Spare time

Use any bits of spare time wisely.

- If you get time to start homework in a lesson, grab the opportunity. You'll have more time for yourself at home then.
- If you travel to school on the train or bus, use the time to review notes, check your planner or revise.

Homework tip

Start your homework with the subject you find most challenging. That way, you will be tackling it when you are fresh.

Be task-focused

Think about each task for a moment before you begin. What are you trying to achieve with it? What is the best way to tackle it?

Time guidelines

You can get an idea of how much time to spend on exam-style questions from the number of marks they are worth.

A very rough guide is that each mark is worth a minute of time.

Examiners' report

"*Keep a close eye on the time during the examination.*" Remember that the front page of the exam paper will tell you how much time you have for the whole exam.

Try it out

You can start to practise thinking this way with all your study tasks. Think about how much a task is worth and set yourself an appropriate time limit to finish it in.

Now try this

Triage is a system of dividing things into three groups according to priority. Try it out with homework tasks. Skim through your tasks and decide (1) which are essential (colour them red), (2) which are important / urgent (yellow) and (3) which are optional / supportive (green). You should then tackle them in this order.

Your time diary

How much time do you have for study? Let's work it out.

How much time do you spend on different activities every day?

Have a think about it and fill in the table below, then add up your totals.

With all the other demands on your time, there actually may not be a huge amount of study time available. That is why you should use it as effectively as possible.

Daily activities

Activity	Hours per day	
Sleeping		
Eating + drinking		
Travelling		Total
Errands / chores		

Errands / chores are things you need to do in the day, such as walking the dog or cleaning your room.

Daily activities + time at school

Activity	Hours per day	
Totals for: Daily activities		Total
Time at school		

Now add in the time you are at school on a typical school day.

This doesn't include time spent travelling to school and back – that is covered in daily activities. But it will include break times.

Put your figure into the table opposite.

Daily activities + time at school + leisure time

Activity	Hours per day	
Totals for: Daily activities		
Time at school		Total
Leisure time		

Now calculate the leisure time you spend every day, doing things you enjoy – watching YouTube, playing sport, doing a hobby, chatting with friends, reading, gaming, etc. Do an average for a typical school day. Put your figure into the table opposite.

There are 24 hours in a day. When you take your grand total (all the above totals added together) from 24 hours, how many hours are left for study time?

On the next page you'll work out when your best study times are in your typical week.

Working out your study times

You know how much study time you have available in an average day, so now you can work out when to use that study time to best effect in an average week.

	Monday	Tuesday	Wednesday	Thursday	Friday
7.00 8.00					
9.00 10.00					
11.00 12.00					
13.00 14.00					
15.00 16.00					
17.00 18.00					
19.00 20.00					
21.00 22.00					

Try it out

In the table above, carry out the following steps.

1 Block out the time you are at school. Either draw a line around this time or shade it in lightly.

2 Block out any times you usually do after-school activities, e.g. football Tuesday 15.30–17.00.

3 Block out time you usually spend on daily activities, such as mealtimes.

4 Now allocate your study time total for each day. Page 27 Use the tips opposite to help.

Tips for allocating study time:
• Spend your study time in 15-minute blocks.
• Try to have your study time at around the same time each day. This helps you get into a regime.
• Think about when your best times for study are. Do you like to get it done early? Do you find it easier to concentrate later in the evening?

What about leisure activities? Study time takes priority, so once you've allocated your study time, you'll see when leisure time fits in.

If you have a lot of after-school commitments, you might be finding it hard to fit enough study time in. The next page has some tips on ways to deal with this.

Now try this

1 Once you have decided when your study times are going to be each day, let the rest of your family know. They should try not to distract you during this time.

2 Give your study timetable a trial run of a week or so and then fine-tune it so it works as well as possible.

3 Make sure you build in rewards to keep you motivated. For example, you could schedule 10–15-minute breaks between bigger blocks of study time.

Protecting your study time

It is important to have a balance of study, leisure and rest but if you find it hard to turn down things that are interrupting your study time, these points should be useful.

Time is valuable

It is difficult to get a good balance between study, leisure and rest if you've got a lot of other commitments, such as different sports clubs, time out with friends or jobs that you've taken on outside school time.

Often, it can be really hard to turn people down when they ask for your time.

> So I can count on you being there? You won't let me down?

> OK, if you really need me …

The power of 'no'

One way to protect your study time is to learn to say 'no'. This will keep you from taking on extra commitments when you already feel overloaded.

This is how you do it.

- Say 'thank you' for being asked and then give an honest explanation of why you have to say 'no'.

- If you are worried about a friend's feelings, work out something you can do together at a later date when you have time to spare.

If you know when your study times are each day and treat that time as 'non-negotiable', that makes it much easier to say 'no' without hesitation.

Block busy time

You can block out time in your planner as busy even if you don't have anything specific to do then.

This is a good way to avoid over-commitment and reminds you to keep a good balance between study, leisure and rest, avoiding unnecessary pressure and stress.

Otherwise you can find that other commitments creep in and, before you know it, you start to feel under pressure.

Now try this

1 Imagine you are being asked to do something you'd be likely to regret taking on. With a friend, role play saying 'no' politely but firmly to the request.

2 Discuss the following with a friend:
- How could you reduce your time commitments to something more manageable? Who might you need to talk to about how to reduce this time?
- How might you steer the conversation?

Using study time productively

Using time productively means getting stuck into a project. But how do you do this when there are so many distractions?

Distractions

Getting stuck into a project can be harder than it sounds.

- You've got urgent homework to do, but someone messages you just as you are finally sitting down to do it.

- Or you suddenly think of something else you need to do, such as get a biscuit or look something up online.

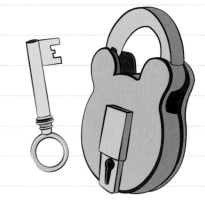

It's true!

In fact, research found that in normal conditions, people work uninterrupted for no longer than about three minutes on average. In addition, people interrupt themselves almost as much as they are interrupted by others.

If you find you can't help wasting time online, there are web services that you can set up to block your access to particular sites for a period of time. But remember to combine this severe approach with rewards for meeting your objectives to keep your motivation up.

Productive chunks

Top tip

Chunking your study time is the best way to study productively. Here is how it works:

- Decide what you are going to study.
- Set the alarm on your phone for 15 minutes from now.
- Do your study task until your alarm goes off.
- Have a break for five minutes.
- Start another 15-minute study chunk.
- Once you have done four chunks, have a longer break – 15 minutes.

Chunking can be very effective if you reward yourself.

Page 9

Try it out

The secret to productive chunking is focus. Your aim in that 15 minutes is to focus on your task and avoid distractions.

- If someone interrupts you, ask them if it is OK if you get back to them after your 15-minute chunk is finished.

- If you interrupt yourself by thinking of something else to do, quickly write that down on a 'to do' list and get back to your study.

- Remember to take your breaks after each chunk, even if you feel like going on studying. The breaks help you to stay motivated and focused.

Now try this

1　What sorts of things interrupt your study time at the moment? How many of them are interruptions from other people (or pets), and how many are distractions you think up for yourself?

2　Try out this technique and decide whether it helped you to use your study time more productively. How could you alter or fine-tune the technique to make it work better for you?

The time management challenge

Here are the time management challenges for your progress tracker. Page 97

1 Grab the opportunity to use three separate spare moments for some productive study, e.g. when a teacher lets you get started on homework in class.

Use this space to describe the three times you grabbed a time opportunity.

Well done.
Add a tick to your progress tracker. ●

2 Use the productive chunking technique for a minimum of one hour's study (4 x 15-minute chunks) and write a review of its strengths and weaknesses.

Page 30

15 minutes

15 minutes   15 minutes

15 minutes

Use this space to record your review findings.
Strengths:

Weaknesses:

Well done.
Add a tick to your progress tracker. ●

3

Calculate how much study time you have and decide how you are going to allocate it throughout a school week.

Pages 27 and 28

Use this space to say how much study time you have a week and how much time you will spend studying on each day of the week.
Study time per week
Monday:
Tuesday:
Wednesday:
Thursday:
Friday:
Well done.
Add a tick to your progress tracker.

Quick quiz

1 How much study time do you have available in a typical week?
2 How long a break should you take after a standard 15-minute chunk?

Points to remember: time management

Time management is about getting the balance right between all the things you do in your life. For students, study time should be a very high-priority activity because study gives you opportunities.

1 Time management is about organising blocks of time so that you maximise your opportunities to learn.

Taking responsibility for your study time and protecting it will mean you minimise the stress of being over-committed.

Top tip

2 Being punctual, keeping to a timetable and completing work on time are basic responsibilities for all students.

Your planner is the key to staying on top of these responsibilities. Keep it up to date and review it regularly.

Top tip

3 With all your other commitments, time at school and daily activities, there may actually be only quite a small amount of study time available each day.

Work out when your study time is each day.

Top tip

4 To make effective use of your time, be clear for each task a) what you are trying to achieve and b) how much of your time it is worth.

There are good techniques to help you focus and avoid distractions.

Top tip

Time management problems

I'll just answer this, then I'll get back to it.

Whenever Molly tries to study, she finds it really hard to concentrate. There always seem to be interruptions or she remembers something really important she has to do.

I've got too much on to get this work done properly – again!

Alex has a lot of commitments already and he finds it very difficult to say 'no' when people ask him to take on something else. So he often has to rush his work to get it done.

Now try this

Using your time management knowledge, what advice would you give Molly and Alex about ways to tackle their study issues? Try to come up with a different suggestion for each student.

What is learning to learn?

There are ways in which you can accelerate your learning and make it more effective. These ways are likely to be quite specific to you. So this chapter is about learning how you learn best.

There are three main stages to making your learning more effective:

1 Setting learning goals.

2 Planning your learning.

3 Reflecting on what you've learned (and testing what you have learned if you are revising).

When you think about how you learn, that's learning to learn.

There are different strategies you can use for each of these three stages.

We'll only look at a few here but there are many more for you to explore.

Objectives

A concept map like this one is an example of a strategy you can use in planning your learning.

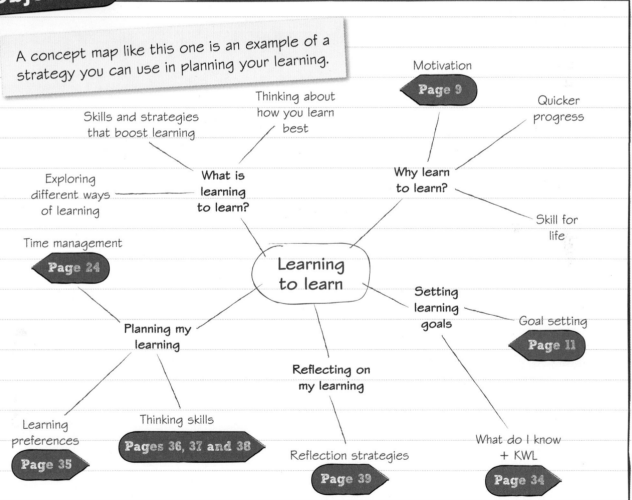

A recent learning to learn project demonstrated a positive impact on students' results, motivation, attendance and behaviour.

Now try this

1 Which page(s) in this chapter has information on thinking skills strategies?

2 Which page tells you about the KWL strategy?

Setting learning goals

The first step of really effective learning is to decide what your goals are for this topic: what is it that you want to know about it?

Chapter 1 introduced goals and objectives.

- Objectives are the steps you complete to reach your goal.

To set a goal for a new topic:

- identify what you already know about a topic
- decide what you want to learn about the new topic
- make that learning happen.

> **Top tip**
>
> Be 100 per cent clear about what you have to do for a topic and how you are going to tackle it.

KWL: Know, Want to know, Learned

This example is for GCSE Geography but you could use this strategy for any subject.

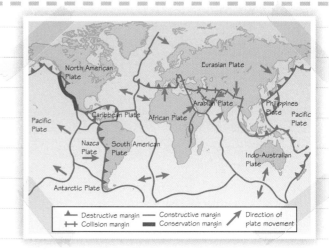

KWL stands for 'Know, Want to know, Learned'. This strategy helps you identify what you already know about a topic, what you want to know and then to record what you've learned.

K	W	L
• Most volcanoes occur along plate boundaries. • Lava and ash from volcanoes can cause major disasters. • There are different types of volcanoes.	• Why do people still live near volcanoes? • What is a supervolcano and what would happen if one erupted now? • Can you predict when a volcano is going to erupt?	• Volcanic soil is very fertile so that's why people still live near them. • Scientists use satellite measurements of ground movements to predict volcanic eruptions.

In the L column you record what you have learned – answers to your questions in the W column. Your goal could be to record answers to all your W questions.

In the K column you write down what you know already. Linking new topics to old ones is a powerful way to achieve effective learning.

In the W column you put what you'd like to know. You can keep adding to this as you go through the topic.

It's true!

In research, this method helped students to focus their reading, looking for particular information and linking it to what they already knew.

Now try this

Try out the KWL strategy for a new topic in one of your subjects. Don't forget to make those links to older topics – and maybe different subjects – as your first step.

Learning approaches

You may find that you like to learn in a particular way. For example, you may like to write down what you are learning. But you probably already use other approaches without even thinking about it. It is worth considering different approaches to learning as some may help you for different subjects.

Visual

Auditory

Read / write

Visual approaches

This is learning by seeing things and by picturing them in your mind. Try:

- looking for the information you need presented as infographics – graphs, maps, diagrams, images, timelines, concept maps or charts – or creating your own
- using bright colours to highlight information and classify different information with colour codes
- using visual cues to help you remember things – associate key terms with mental images.

Auditory approaches

Your listening skills can help you learn. Try:

- accessing podcasts about your topic and video clips of people speaking about it, and take notes
- listening to songs to help you learn language vocabulary, rules, equations or facts
- discussing what you are working on with a partner, setting up group discussions about your topic, recording your own presentation about your topic.

Read / write approaches

These are about information presented in writing. Try:

- putting information into lists, compiling your own definitions of key terms
- making your own notes for everything, making sure there are clear headings for each section
- accessing textbook explanations, online information sources, teacher handouts
- processing diagrams, charts, etc. into written descriptions, e.g. 'this graph shows that ...'
- remembering things by writing them out several times.

What works for you?

Varying your approaches can be useful when you have a lot to learn, for example when you revise.

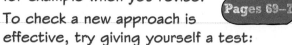

Pages 69–75

To check a new approach is effective, try giving yourself a test:

- Give yourself a topic to learn and half an hour to learn it.
- Test yourself straight afterwards.
- Test yourself in three days' time.

If you can't remember the material, it might be that the technique isn't effective for you or for that topic, or that you need to practise again – give yourself another chance.

Now try this

Imagine you wanted to analyse the character of Lady Macbeth in Shakespeare's play *Macbeth*. How could you tap into each of these learning approaches to help you with this task?

Thinking skills: coming up with ideas

Planning how you are going to learn involves planning what specific strategies to use to get the best results. There are lots of different strategies you can use – the three on this page relate to generating ideas.

1 Focused listing

In this technique, you list what you can recall about a topic – a list of terms and ideas that are related to it.

For example, for a focused list for the topic of photosynthesis, you might list:

- chlorophyll
- green plants
- carbon dioxide
- light energy
- glucose
- oxygen.

2 Brainstorming

In brainstorming, you write down everything you can think of about a topic. Anything is permissible – try not to think whether something is good or not, just write it down.

Brainstorming can produce some very creative approaches to problems, as long as you just let the ideas come.

Brainstorming on your own often produces more creative results than in a group. Why do you think that might be?

3 Ideas funnel

The ideas funnel follows on from brainstorming and helps you prioritise your ideas.

- Pick the five ideas you think are the best / most relevant from your brainstormed ideas.
- You should be able to justify why you've picked those five.
- If you need to, you can then funnel it down further. Out of those five, pick the best / most relevant one.

You can also use concept maps to unpick the connections between ideas.

Page 37

Now try this

1 Brainstorm your ideas about this subject, or choose a different issue that you find more interesting if you prefer: 'Ways I could reward myself for doing well in my exams.'

2 Use the ideas funnel to help you prioritise your ideas to the best five and then the single best idea.

3 Now reflect on your learning. What did you find useful about the strategies? What were the difficulties and how might you adapt the strategies to improve them for the way you like to learn?

Thinking skills: developing ideas

Concept maps help you develop ideas, see connections between them, consider different sides to them and consider them from more than one point of view. Concept maps are useful tools for planning your learning.

Concept mapping

- Put your topic or issue or question in the middle of a big piece of paper.
- Draw out 'branches' from the central topic to important categories of the topic.
- From those important categories, draw out 'sub-branches' to individual facts or ideas that connect to them.

You can see how this works in the pictures.

Top tip

Tips for useful concept maps:
- Use images to bring the map to life.
- Use colours to colour-code categories.
- Keep the text simple, use key words.

You can use concept maps for revision and to map out the different topics you need to cover as well as for organising your own ideas or ideas you come up with in a group.

Ideas funnel

The ideas funnel can help with identifying categories for a concept map. Page 36

- Start with a brainstorm about the topic.
- Then read through all your ideas, looking for connections between them.
- You could circle the ideas that fit together in the same colour.
- Then use the ideas funnel to write down names for each group of ideas.

① Put the title of the topic you are exploring in the middle of the page.

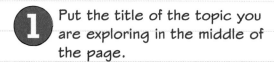

② Add in the main categories.

③ Keep drawing more connections until your map is complete.

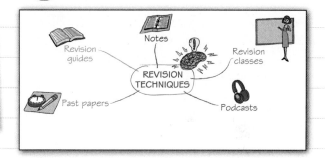

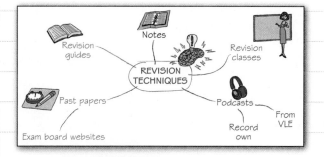

Examiners' report

Examiners report that the most successful longer written answers (essay-style) have usually been planned. Planning (you could sometimes use a concept map to plan) gives longer answers a clear structure and helps with answers requiring a judgement that is supported all the way through.

Now try this

Draw a concept map to organise your ideas about one of the following.
- Apps that could help your study skills.
- Places you would like to visit.
- Things that help you to concentrate.

Thinking skills: evaluating ideas

Evaluating means working out how valuable something is. We usually do that by weighing up its advantages and disadvantages, good points and bad points, positives and negatives.

1 Plus – Minus – Interesting

This strategy helps you see different sides to an issue. That is much better than just putting down a 'knee-jerk' reaction – the first thing you think of.

- Plus = a benefit of the issue, something good about it.
- Minus = a downside or disadvantage of the issue.
- Interesting = something you find interesting about the issue.

Take offshore wind farms, for example. Plus = wind farms generate renewable energy. Minus = they only work when it is windy. Interesting = the world's biggest offshore wind farm is Hornsea One, off the Yorkshire coast in the North Sea.

2 SWOT

SWOT stands for Strengths, Weaknesses, Opportunities, Threats.

- Strengths and Weaknesses are the same as the plus and minus of Plus – Minus – Interesting.
- Opportunities and Threats are about the future: What good things could happen? What problems might occur?

SWOTs are done in a matrix like this:

Strengths	Weaknesses
Opportunities	Threats

Here's an example of a SWOT for a D&T project.

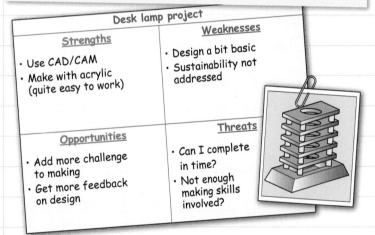

Desk lamp project

Strengths
- Use CAD/CAM
- Make with acrylic (quite easy to work)

Weaknesses
- Design a bit basic
- Sustainability not addressed

Opportunities
- Add more challenge to making
- Get more feedback on design

Threats
- Can I complete in time?
- Not enough making skills involved?

Two advanced skills are often needed to access high marks in GCSE questions.

Top tip

- Analysing information: breaking concepts up into the parts that make them up. A concept map is a good tool for this.
- Evaluating information: making a judgement about something – being able to weigh up strengths against weaknesses.

Now try this

1 Use the Plus – Minus – Interesting technique to evaluate the idea that school summer holidays should only be three weeks long.

2 Use the SWOT technique to evaluate this business idea: students who did well in their GCSEs get paid to help year 11 students get ready for their exams via online video tutorials.

Reflecting on your learning

Reflecting on your learning is the third stage of learning to learn. It is about looking back on what you have done.

You can reflect on a task as you are doing it and also when it is completed.

- As you go through a task, it is useful to keep track of how you are getting on.
- Reflecting on a task once you've completed it helps you make sense of what you've achieved and how you might tackle something similar in the future. When you are revising, it will also help you to consider whether you remember what you have learnt.

There are lots of different ways of reflecting on your work.

- Keep a learning journal to record learning strategies that worked well for you.
- Discuss with other students what you're doing and how it is going.
- Use self-assessment forms and checklists to structure your reflection.

Some reflection questions

These questions are linked to the idea of there being three levels of learning. You can use as many of them as you like to help you reflect on any learning project, or come up with your own list.

What did I already know about this topic when we began it?	What did we find out that was surprising to me or unexpected?
What links with other topics or subjects did I discover?	How could I find more links? And how could I record them?
What did I want to find out about this topic?	What did we not cover that I expected we would?
What were the three main things I learned from this topic?	What did we find out about that I would like to study in more detail?
What am I unsure about in this topic?	How could I improve my understanding of the things I'm not sure about?
How accurate was I at estimating how long different tasks for this topic would take?	How could I improve my time management skills for similar tasks in the future?
What learning approaches did we use in finding out about this topic?	What learning approaches did I find most effective, and why?
What thinking skills strategies did we use in learning about this topic?	Which strategies did I find most effective, and why?
What parts of this topic did I find challenging?	What did I do about these challenges and how could I improve what I do next time?
How motivated and engaged with this topic did I feel?	How could I increase my motivation for studying this topic and my engagement with this topic?
What have I learned about the way I learn best?	What would I do differently next time?

It's true!

Students who reflect on their learning become more independent, motivated learners.

Now try this

Try keeping a learning journal. It could be in a notebook or as a blog, or anything you like, but the point of it is to record new knowledge, skills or understanding and your thoughts about them.

39

The learning to learn challenge

Here are the learning to learn challenge tasks for your progress tracker. **Page 97**

1 Try out the KWL strategy next time you start a new topic in one of your subjects. **Page 34**

K	W	L

Use this space to reflect on the KWL strategy: how useful you found it and whether you'd use it again.

Well done.
Add a tick to your progress tracker. ⬤

2 Use at least three different learning approaches within the same school day. **Page 35**

You can use them all in the same piece of work or in different pieces of work. If you can't quite fit them into one day it still counts.

Use this space to reflect on which learning approach proved to be the most effective and why you think that was.

Well done.
Add a tick to your progress tracker. ⬤

3 Keep a learning journal for two weeks, noting what strategies you have used in your learning and how effective they have been.

Record how it felt when you were learning something and anything you noticed about what else was happening at the same time: where were you, what was happening around you, what sort of format was the information you were learning from, e.g. a book, a presentation …? Recreating these feelings / situations could possibly help you next time you are studying.

You can keep your journal any way you like: as a blog, as drawings and sketches, recorded as video or audio – anything.

Use this space to identify the things that help you learn and the things that are obstacles to your learning effectively.

Helps me:

Obstacles:

Well done.
Add a tick to your progress tracker.

Quick quiz

1 What does SWOT stand for?

2 One of Shakespeare's plays is mentioned in this chapter. Which one?

Points to remember: learning to learn

Learning to learn is about accelerating your learning and making it more effective. How you like to learn will be quite specific to you, although it is worth continuing to explore other ways of learning in case they prove to be more effective.

1 Learning to learn is about becoming aware of how you like to learn, and exploring whether there are other ways of learning that might also work for you.

Like a lot of the skills in this book, learning to learn is based on you taking an active role in deciding what and how you are learning.

Top tip

2 The first step is to identify what you already know about a topic and what you would like to know.

Linking new topics to ones you've already studied makes for very effective learning. Deciding what you want to learn is very motivating for study.

3 The second step is to plan your learning – make a plan for how you are going to approach a learning task.

This involves planning how much time to give it, the thinking approaches you'll use and the steps you'll take to complete the task.

4 The third step is to reflect on your learning, and evaluate how effective it has been.

Reflective learners are able to identify what went well and what didn't go so well. They can make good decisions about how to tackle similar projects in the future.

Now try this

Read these statements and decide if they are examples of learning to learn or not.

1. I try to relate new topics to topics we've done before in this subject and in others.

2. I keep my head down and get through the work as fast as possible.

3. We have so much work to do that I feel under pressure; it is stressful.

4. Some topics are easy but some I just don't get at all. With any luck, just the easy ones will come up in the exam.

5. Now I've found out that I can do my homework in the library without any interruptions, I'm doing much better than when I tried to do it at home.

6. My motivation is to get the best possible grades in my subjects. I like to find out what exam questions are likely to focus on for each topic that we cover.

7. Keeping a learning journal has been very useful. It makes a lot of sense to me to find out the ways that I learn best.

8. It is the teacher's job to make topics interesting for me. That is what they are paid for.

9. Every week we have a test and every week I get most of the answers right. I've got a good memory for facts.

10. When I get stuck on a problem, I switch learning approaches and that sometimes helps me find a different way through it.

Introducing speaking and listening skills

Most people do the majority of their learning through listening and discussing, so speaking and listening skills are really worth developing. Here is what this chapter will cover.

Objectives

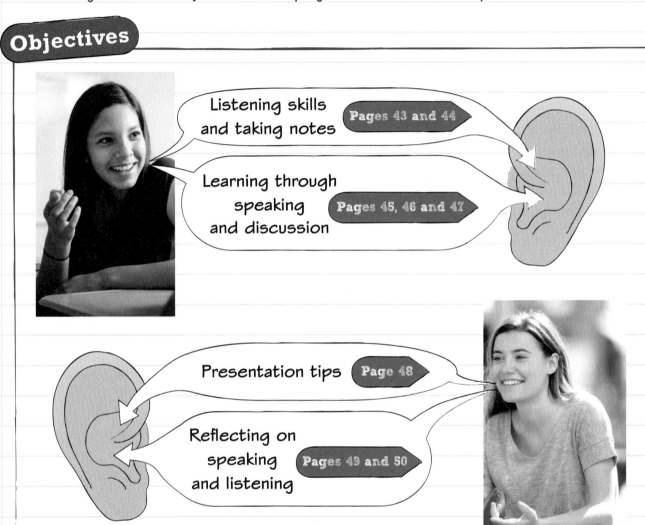

Listening skills and taking notes   **Pages 43 and 44**

Learning through speaking and discussion   **Pages 45, 46 and 47**

Presentation tips   **Page 48**

Reflecting on speaking and listening   **Pages 49 and 50**

It's true!

Adults spend an average of 70% of their time engaged in some sort of communication. Of this, an average of 45% is spent listening compared to 30% speaking, 16% reading and 9% writing. So it is really important to use that time wisely!

Now try this

1   Which pages of this chapter would help you remember what you have listened to by taking notes?

2   Which page of this chapter will give you ideas to improve your presentations?

How to listen

The key to learning a lot by listening to someone is to get involved. This is connected to learning to learn. Identify what you know already, decide what else you want to learn and then make that learning happen. Page 33

Key word bingo

How to play:

- List the key terms you think will come up in a lesson.
- Each time someone in the class uses one, cross it off your list and score 10.
- If a key term is used that you don't have, add it to your list.
- If you use a key term yourself in something you say in the lesson, score 20.

Key word bingo is good for learning but make sure your teacher is OK with you playing it first.

The best way not to be bored in lessons is to get yourself motivated to learn.

Mindfulness

You can train your awareness to focus on the present. See Chapter 10 for some introductory practices to see if this could help you.

Top tip

It's true!

Body language

Research has shown that body language has an impact on how we feel. This is especially true for smiling, which makes you happier – even if it isn't a 'real' smile. Try it!

To get in the right position for paying attention:

- uncross your arms
- sit with a straight back
- smile.

These body language signals also show the person who is talking to you that you are interested in what they are saying.

Examiners' report

"Candidates need to listen to the whole rather than just home in on individual items of vocabulary."

You will need good listening skills for modern languages listening papers. Remember to listen to the whole section to help you answer correctly.

Make connections between what you hear and:

- something you've already studied
- something relevant to you
- a real-life example / a real-life application.

Good listening skills are closely linked to taking notes. There is advice on taking notes on the next page.

Now try this

Some people find it easier to learn from what they hear rather than what they see. Look for some reliable podcasts on a subject you enjoy and see if 'listening to learn' works for you.

Taking notes

Making good notes is tricky but very important. As you listen, you need to translate what you hear into something you can write down quickly, in a way that will be useful to you later. Here's how to set up a page to take really good notes.

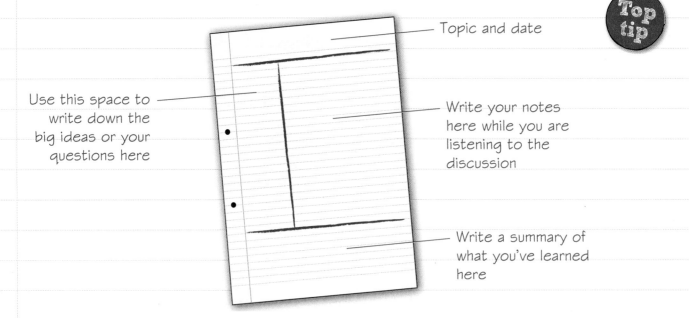

Top tip

Topic and date

Use this space to write down the big ideas or your questions here

Write your notes here while you are listening to the discussion

Write a summary of what you've learned here

This way of making notes is good because it encourages you to think about questions and to reflect on what you've learned.

If you put your notes into your folder then you'll be able to find them again next time you need them. Page 16

Using handouts

What if your teacher has given you a handout that summarises what they are talking about? Do you still need to make notes?

Yes! The handout tells you the key information already, so you don't need to write too much. But now your notes can be reflective and include:

- your personal views and comments
- questions you'd like to ask
- things you are not sure about.

Notes on PowerPoint presentations

If your teacher is using a PowerPoint presentation for a lesson, then you will probably be able to get a copy of it from the VLE or as a printout.

PowerPoint presentations often make a lot less sense on their own compared to when a teacher is explaining them!

- Add your notes to your copy while you can still remember the lesson.
- Encourage your teachers to record narrations to their presentations.

Now try this

1 Research says it is better to listen and then summarise key points in your notes rather than just trying to record what someone is saying word for word. Why do you think that is?

2 You can speed up your note-taking by coming up with **abbreviations** for things teachers commonly say. For example, use RFT for revise for test. What other abbreviations would come in handy? Consider whether you need subject-specific abbreviations too.

Asking questions

Answering questions is a big part of being involved in your lessons – teachers need to check you've understood and find out what you think about things. Asking your own questions is the next step up.

Reporter's questions

Top tip

The 'reporter's questions' are who?, what?, when?, where?, why? and how? Use these to help you set up effective questions as in the following examples.

- What do I already know about this?
- Who would be a good discussion partner for this topic?
- Where can I find out more information?
- When is the deadline for this?
- Why do we need to know this?
- How might the exam paper ask an exam question about this?

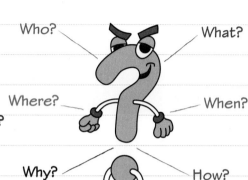

Exam questions

Exam papers ask questions that step up in difficulty.

- Questions that ask you to 'state' or 'name' are often asking what something is.
- Questions that ask you to 'describe' are asking for you to give details about something: who?, what?, where?, when?
- Questions that ask you to 'explain' something are asking about 'why?' and 'how?' For example, 'What are the reasons?'
- Questions involving evaluation are like explanation questions plus reflection. For example, 'How far do you agree ...?'

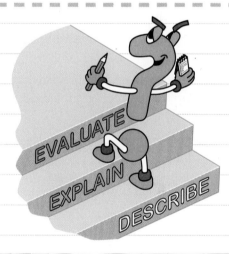

You can ask your own exam-style questions about a topic in class.

- Could you say what is meant by that term?
- Could you describe the differences between those two again, please?
- Please could you explain how that works and why it is different from the first example?
- Which of those theories do you think is better?

There isn't always a good time to ask questions in class. Your school may run after-school study clubs, or you could suggest to your teachers that they set up an email address that you can use to ask questions.

The best way to learn is to find out the answer for yourself.

Now try this

1 If you could ask anyone from the past or in the present three questions, who would you ask and what would you ask them?

2 Do you know the difference between open questions and closed questions? (That was a closed question.) Why do you think teachers like to ask open questions? (That was an open question.)

Group discussions

Some subjects have a lot of group work and group discussions. How do you make group discussions work for you?

Group discussion ground rules

Top tip

- Pay close attention to what others say.
- No butting in: wait until the other person has finished speaking.
- Ask questions to develop ideas.
- Encourage everyone in the group to participate.
- Reflect on the process: what could the group do better next time?

Why group discussions are useful

- You all build up your understanding together.
- It is easier to ask questions and try out ideas than with the whole class listening.
- Other people have different strengths that you can learn from.
- Other people's perspectives make it easier to see different sides of a question.

Group discussion problems

- One person doing all the talking.
- Running out of time.
- Discussions that go off track.
- Feeling like you haven't got anything to say or no one is listening.

Group discussion roles

Coordinator – aware of priorities, encourages others, delegates tasks.

Plant – creative, imaginative and original. Solves difficult problems.

Shaper – challenges the group to overcome difficulties.

Teamworker – works well with others, listens and helps people get along.

Implementer – turns ideas into practical actions.

Specialist – provides specialist knowledge and skills that others in the group don't have.

Roles within a group

Completer Finisher – ensures work is done to a high standard.

Resource Investigator – explores opportunities and making new contacts.

Monitor Evaluator – weighs up all options and new ideas without emotion. Judges accurately.

These roles come from the research and work of Dr Meredith Belbin.

If your group discussions are getting stuck, think about what might be missing. For example, does someone need to act as a coordinator to get the discussion back on track? Could you take on that role, or encourage someone else to?

Now try this

1. Think of the people in your classes or study groups. Can you find an example of a person to fit with each of the different roles on this page?

2. Describe an example of a group project you have been part of that worked really well, and one that didn't work so well. Why do you think one was successful and the other wasn't?

Group discussion strategies

Working in groups can be a challenge when everyone in the group has different ideas about what you should do. However, you can channel these differences into something really creative using these strategies.

> If you feel a group discussion is getting bogged down, use these strategies to get it moving again.

Generator

The generator strategy is to come up with as many ideas as possible, no matter how weird some might be. It doesn't matter at this stage if the ideas would work or not.

Use the generator strategy to get over the problem of many group discussions where people are afraid to put ideas forward in case they just get shot down.

Summary as courtesy

One problem with group discussions is that people don't always listen to other people's views properly.

With this strategy, you can only say what you want to say once you have correctly summarised the point that the previous group member made.

Question quest

One way of encouraging people to say more is to ask them questions. The question quest strategy asks each member of the group to come up with a question they want answered about the task you are discussing.

This strategy can help everyone in the group feel more involved in the discussion objectives.

Six Thinking Hats

This strategy, created by famous creative thinker Edward de Bono, gives groups six imaginary hats that each represent a different way of thinking: feelings, information, optimistic thinking, careful thinking, creativity and reflective thinking.

The group can 'put on' different hats to help you look at your task from six different perspectives.

Jigsaw

Use this strategy for big group tasks. Instead of everyone in the group trying to work through everything together, divide the job up. Then everyone shares the main points of what they've done or found out with the group as a whole.

If you are in a big group, you could work in pairs rather than on your own. It is helpful to have someone to share ideas and questions with.

> Try out all of these group discussion strategies and see which ones are effective for you.

Now try this

Find out more about the **Six Thinking Hats** strategy. How would you use this strategy to help discussions? Would you start with everyone 'putting on' a blue hat to make sure the project objectives were clearly set out? Or getting creative with green-hat thinking? Or would different people 'wear' each of the hats so that you got a range of viewpoints? How long would you recommend people 'wore' a hat for? Develop some guidelines.

Presentation tips

There are a few pitfalls to avoid when you are presenting to the rest of your class, but the good news is they are very easy to avoid with a bit of planning and rehearsal.

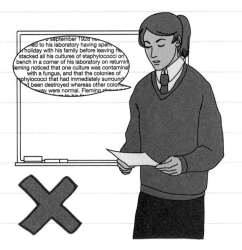

Preparing your presentation

Top tip

✗ Don't just print off an article on your topic and read it out to the class.

✓ Do your presentation properly. Decide what information you need to get across to help everyone in your class or group understand this topic. Explain it clearly.

✓ Try to use notes just to prompt you rather than to read from. Look up and make eye contact with your audience.

Presenting as a group

Top tip

✓ If you are in a group presentation, have at least one run-through of your presentation. That way you can be sure of who says what and when.

✓ It's a really good idea for each speaker to hand over to the next one. For example: 'I'm now going to hand on to Abi, who is going to tell you about how antibiotics were discovered.'

✓ If you are doing a presentation on your own, it is still a really good idea to rehearse it.

Presentation of information

Top tip

✗ Don't cram information onto each presentation screen and then read it out.

✓ Instead, use bullet points on screen to summarise your key points, and expand on them in what you say.

✓ Use a large font size (30 point) so your text is easy to read from the back of the room.

✓ Use an image that connects directly to the point you want to make on each slide.

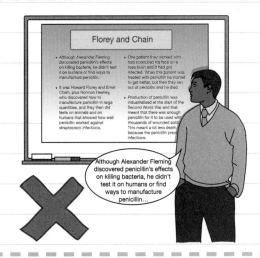

Now try this

Put together a presentation on planning and delivering a good presentation. Use the following as titles for your slides: Make it clear, Keep it simple, Make it visual, Don't just read it, Don't rush through it, Enjoy it.

The speaking and listening challenge

Here are the speaking and listening challenge tasks for your progress tracker. **Page 97**

1 Play key word bingo in one or more of your subjects and reach a score of 100 or over.
Remember to check **Page 43**
with your teacher first
before playing key word bingo.

Use this space to write down the key words that gave you your winning score.

Well done.
Add a tick to your progress tracker. ●

2 In any lesson in any subject, write down three things you would like to know about the topic you are covering.

Ask one of your questions. All of them, if you like.

Use this space to write down the question you asked and the answer you received.

Well done.
Add a tick to your progress tracker. ●

3 Use a learning journal approach to record your experiences of being in discussions **Page 39**
in your subjects.

These can be whole-class discussions, discussions in groups or in pairs.

What things helped you learn from discussions? What strategies did you find useful in listening to discussions? What strategies helped you ask questions in discussions? What strategies were used to help make discussions more productive, and how well did they work?

Use this space to record the top three things that help you get the most out of discussions.

A

B

C

Well done.
Add a tick to your progress tracker. ●

Quick quiz

1 Is this an open question?
2 Which thinking strategy involves an item of clothing?

Points to remember: speaking and listening

Students often ask teachers 'why do we need to know this?' It is a good question. A really good teacher will answer with a question of their own – 'Why do you think you need to know this?'

1 Listening doesn't seem as important as speaking – but it is. Here's a quote from Larry King, a TV host who has interviewed thousands of famous people:

'I remind myself every morning: Nothing I say this day will teach me anything. So if I'm going to learn, I must do it by listening.'

2 Rather than thinking about what you want to say in a discussion, think about what you could ask.

The 'reporter's questions' are very useful for thinking of what to ask – Who?, What?, Where?, When?, Why? and How? Questions starting 'why?' and 'how?' can open up explanations and evaluations.

3 Presentations can feel like they are all about you: a performance on a stage.

In fact, presentations are not just about you. They are about your audience. How can you make your presentation clear and interesting for them?

4 Group discussions are one of the best ways to learn about anything. This is because you learn so much more when you are really involved.

It is worthwhile working out how you can get the most from group discussions and what strategies help best with this.

Now try this

1 Use this picture to show a common problem caused by people not listening properly. Do this by filling in the thought and speech bubbles.

2 Now give the people in the photo some advice on improving their speaking and listening skills.

Research skills

Finding answers involves developing effective research skills and reading skills. Research skills are key to helping you find the information you are looking for and reading skills help you find the answers to your questions.

Objectives

Web Email Photos Groups ▼

| Study skills book+"Chapter 6"+"Your objectives" | Search |

Search complete: 6 results in 0.1 seconds

How to organise your research
How a simple plan can make research easier to handle.   Page 52

Internet research skills
Ways to make internet searches more precise, which saves you time and effort.   Page 53

SQ3R
SQ3R stands for Survey, Questions and 3Rs –
Read, Recall, Review. It is an 'active reading' technique that helps you learn a lot more from what you read.   Page 54

Taking notes
This method of taking notes supports the SQ3R technique and also produces valuable resources for revision.   Page 55

Academic honesty
Academic honesty is about expressing things your own way rather than copying other people, and about acknowledging when you've used the work or ideas of someone else.   Page 56

Online research tools
These free online tools may be useful in helping you find answers to your questions.   Page 57

It's true!

Studies have found that research can be much faster and more effective if you first plan exactly what you want to find.

Now try this

1   What are the 3Rs in the SQ3R reading technique?
2   Which page of this chapter will help you to find information online more quickly and precisely?

How to organise your research

There are many different sources of information available, especially on the internet. It is easy to waste a lot of time following one link to another. It is much better to have a clear plan for achieving your research goal.

Whatever you are researching, it helps to have a method.

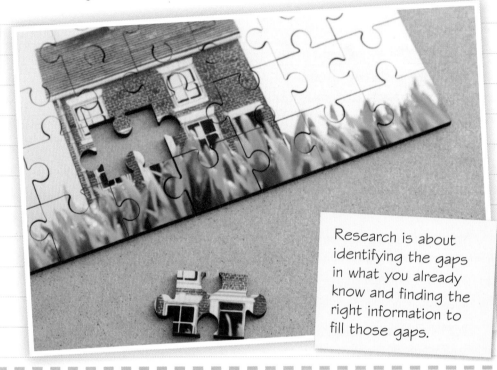

Research is about identifying the gaps in what you already know and finding the right information to fill those gaps.

The research process

- How long have you got to do this research?
- Plan a schedule (what needs to be done by when).
- Keep to your schedule to meet the deadline.

- Select just the information that's relevant to your research goal.
- Summarise the info: put it into your own words rather than copying it word for word.
- Make sure you record the source of the info so you can find it again if you need to.

 1 Define your research goal ➡   **2** Check your deadline ➡ **3** Locate your sources ➡   **4** Select, summarise, source

- What do you already know about this topic?
- What exactly do you need to find out?
- How much info do you need?

- What are the best sources of information to go to for this research goal?
- Consider a range of sources – e.g. school library as well as the internet!

Now try this

Try this method out with the following research task: What is the oldest book in your school library?

Internet research skills

Most of us may not be searching the internet very efficiently. These tips are designed to help with that.

Advanced search

Searching on a single word will often produce millions of hits. You need to narrow things down as much as you can.

- Think carefully about your search terms. Subject-specific key terms may produce more specific results.

- Search for a phrase by typing it inside "double quote marks". That way, you'll search for all those words in that same order.

- Combine search terms by using the plus sign (+). For example: fish +chips. Don't leave any space between the + and the second search term – try it and see why.

- Use the minus sign (−) to exclude something from your search. Like with +, don't leave any space between the − and the second term, e.g. geography −maps.

- To search for results within a specific site, include the symbol : followed by the site name in your query. For example: revision:bbc.co.uk

- Most search engines let you limit your search to just UK pages – that's really helpful since so many English-language sites are from the US.

- You can also filter your search. For example, with Google you can search just for results from Google Books or Blogger or Groups – and many more. Click on Search tools to find these.

- Use two full stops to search within a specific range, e.g. Olympics 2012..2020.

- Remember that the more terms you include in your search, the more specific your results will be.

There are a lot of other options to explore.

[   ] [Search]

It's true!

Although we think of searching the internet as a trivial skill, because we do it every day, studies have found that we don't always do it very efficiently.

Now try this

1. A student from the UK needs to revise for a GCSE Maths exam: Foundation Tier.
   Suggest the search terms the student should use.

2. A student with an egg allergy is looking for a sponge cake recipe.
   How could they do a search for recipes that exclude eggs?

3. A student needs to read a section from *Macbeth* for their homework, but has forgotten to bring their copy home.
   What's a quick way to find a free online copy (using a search engine)?

4. A student needs to find out by how much the world population increased between 1970 and 1990.
   What would be a good way to set out their search terms?

SQ3R

SQ3R is a popular reading method that will supercharge the effectiveness of your reading and research. S stands for Survey, Q stands for Questions and the three Rs are Read, Recall, Review.

Top tip

Survey

Survey means taking an overview of what you are about to read.

- Skim through any headings to get a quick idea of what is covered.
- Read the first paragraph of the chapter or section.
- Read headings for any charts or diagrams, read picture captions.
- Read the last paragraph.

Spend about five minutes on your survey. It will make reading faster and more productive because you will already know a lot about what is coming up.

Questions

As you are surveying, ask yourself questions. Here are some examples.

- Why is this important?
- What questions is the author trying to answer?
- How does the information here help me achieve my research goal? **Page 52**
- What is interesting or unusual about this?

Use the 'reporter's questions' to help you think of what to ask the text. **Page 45**

Read, Recall, Review

As you read, search for answers to your questions. Don't stop to make notes as you read.

Recall: once you've finished reading a section, pause. Ask yourself your questions and say out loud the answers that you've found in that section, putting them into your own words. This is a good point to make notes (see next page).

Review: cover your notes and in your head go back over what you read and the answers you got for your questions. This helps you to really understand and remember the information.

If you get to a section of text that is hard to understand, slow right down and take it bit by bit.

It's very important to put answers into your own words. This gets your brain fully engaged with its favourite task, which is looking for **meanings**.

Reading with your questions in mind (or written down on a list beside you) helps you keep your focus. It is also motivating because you are reading with a purpose.

Now try this

Have a go at the SQ3R method for yourself. It works with online sources and with books and other printed sources of information.

There's lots more information about the method online (including SQ3R worksheets) to help you get to grips with this method of active reading.

Now I'll write down the answer to that question using my own words.

SQ3R and taking notes

Earlier you were introduced to a method for taking notes when you are listening to something. You can also combine this same method with SQ3R. Here's how you adapt this method of taking notes to work with SQ3R:

Page 44

1 Source details (name of book, web address of web page)

2 Your questions

3 Your notes. These should be done in the **recall** stage, not while you are reading. Use your own words

4 Write a summary of what you've learned here

---

5 Once you have written notes, you can fold the page in half like this to do the review stage of SQ3R:

What is aseptic surgery?

When was it invented?

Who invented it?

Why was it better than antiseptic?

Keep your notes safe because this way of taking notes produces very useful revision resources too. Fold back the notes so you can just see your questions, and see how much of your answers you can remember.

Leave plenty of space between the points you make in your notes. Chunks of information are much easier to process than masses of text.

It's true!

SQ3R was invented by an American professor during World War II to help soldiers get to grips with lots of very technical information.

Now try this

Try this note-taking method out and evaluate its strengths and weaknesses. What **enhancements** would you make to the system so it works better for you?

Academic honesty

What is academic honesty? It's about expressing your own thoughts and creative thinking, and about acknowledging when you've used the work or ideas of someone else. If you use the work of other people without doing this, then this is called plagiarism.

How to be authentic

If you represent yourself authentically, it means you aren't faking.

There are two sides to being authentic.

1 Be true to yourself.

2 Give credit to others when you use their ideas.

Being true to yourself

If you set up an account on social media with all sorts of new achievements and a photo that looked a lot like someone else, you wouldn't be surprised if your friends wondered what you were up to.

You want your online identity to represent the best of you, but you still want it to express the real you.

Research and academic honesty

When you are researching information to use in your own work, it's very important to:

- relate what you read to your own questions and to your own research goal
- make notes that summarise key points from the source using your own words
- acknowledge (credit) other people's work when you use it – say who wrote it and where it comes from.

Academic honesty also means not cheating in exams, not doing work for another student or copying another student's work and making out it is your work.

Avoiding plagiarism

Get into the habit of recording sources for your research, e.g. the URL of a web page, the title of a book.

The SQ3R technique of active reading provides a good framework for always taking notes using your own words.

Teachers can use special computer programs to check work for plagiarism. The most common one is called Turnitin.

Turnitin describes three of the most frequent and problematic types of plagiarism as follows.

1 Clone: when students use someone else's work word for word as their own.

2 CTRL-C: using big chunks from a single source without any changes.

3 Mashup: mixing up material that's copied word for word from multiple sources.

Now try this

It is possible to spot plagiarism fairly easily. Try identifying other ways in which students sometimes try to pass off other people's work as their own.

Search for Turnitin +"The Plagiarism Spectrum" for the complete top-ten list.

Online research tools

There are lots of free online tools you can use to help organise your research and make it more productive.

Search tools

Google is most people's first choice of search engine, but you should try a few others, such as:

- DuckDuckGo – this search engine does not track your search terms and pass them on to advertisers
- Sweet Search – experts evaluate every search result
- Bing – lets you preview a bit of the page for each search result.

Online encyclopedias

There are other online encyclopedias you could check out as well as Wikipedia, such as:

- HowStuffWorks – aims to provide simple explanations for ... how stuff works
- Encyclopaedia Britannica Online – you can trust this to be accurate
- CIA World Factbook – reliable information on every country in the world.

Simple English Wikipedia is also worth a look when you don't want as much detail as Wikipedia itself.

Online dictionaries can be really useful for words you aren't sure about, for example The Free Dictionary.

Organising sources

It's difficult to keep track of everything interesting that you find on the internet. Tools such as Evernote and Pinterest can help to solve this problem.

Once you've subscribed to them, you can easily save links and organise them into different topics.

Social bookmarking tools also let you access links collected by other people interested in the same topics.

Collaborative tools

If you are working as a group on a project, you can use tools such as Google Drive or Dropbox to help. You have to sign up for an account but they are free.

Instead of everyone going away and working on their own, these collaborative tools mean you can all work on the same document at the same time.

It's also easy to see who did what.

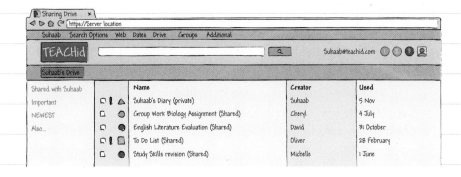

Now try this

Pick a topic you are interested in from your studies and compare what different search engines find for it. Try a range of different engines – and perhaps find a new favourite!

The finding answers challenge

Here are the finding answers challenge tasks for your progress tracker. Page 97

1 Complete an internet search (any topic) using three of the tips for more effective searches. Use a different search engine from your usual one.

Pages 53 and 57

Use this space to record the three tips you used. Give each a score out of five for how much they helped you find what you needed.

1 | 1 | 2 | 3 | 4 | 5 |

2 | 1 | 2 | 3 | 4 | 5 |

3 | 1 | 2 | 3 | 4 | 5 |

Well done.
Add a tick to your progress tracker.

2 Use the SQ3R method to read about a topic from a school textbook (choose a topic you are studying) and take notes. *Pages 54 and 55*

Reflect on your experience. How different is it from how you usually read and take notes?

Use this space for a brief summary of your reflection.

Well done.
Add a tick to your progress tracker.

3 Look back at a topic you studied last term. Evaluate the notes and handouts that you have for this topic.

1 Are there any gaps in your notes where you missed lessons?

2 Are the notes well organised so it is easy to find what you need?

3 Do your notes and the handouts still make sense to you?

4 Is the information on the notes and handouts familiar to you or not?

Decide on ways you could improve your note-taking and how you store your notes.

Use this space to write what you are going to do differently to improve the way you record and store what you've found out about a topic.

Well done.
Add a tick to your progress tracker.

Quick quiz

1 What does SQ3R stand for?

2 Which page mentions fish and chips?

Points to remember: finding answers

The internet has made finding answers to things both easier and harder. The key to finding answers from any source of information is being very clear about the questions you are asking.

1 Setting a research goal will make research much easier.

The internet makes searching very easy, but finding what you need can be a very long and frustrating process. A research goal helps you be clear about what you are looking for and the steps you'll take in order to find it.

2 Like all effective learning, you can take control of your reading and research by deciding what *you* want to learn.

Ask your own questions and use your skills to find your own answers. You will learn more and feel more motivated.

3 It is important to use your own words to summarise what you've found out about a topic.

Using your own words triggers your brain to look for meanings and connections. You will understand more and be more likely to remember it.

4 Your own take on a topic is much more interesting to you and your teachers than copying what someone else says.

Academic honesty is about saying what you think and also about giving other people credit for their ideas when these have helped you.

Now try this

Put the following statements into your own words.

1 'What's in a name? That which we call a rose by any other name would smell as sweet.'

2 All life on Earth has a common ancestor.

3 'A lie gets halfway around the world before the truth has a chance to get its pants on.'

My versions:

Writing: an introduction

Writing is a very important part of learning because it is when you bring together the things you have learned and explain what they mean to you. Study skills for writing help you do yourself justice in your written work. Since most of your exams will depend on written work, these are important skills to learn.

You will do different types of writing for different subjects and for different types of projects. For any kind of writing, think of GAPS.

Top tip

Genre – e.g. an essay, a blog post, a story.

Audience – who you are writing it for.

Purpose – what you are writing it for.

Style – e.g. exam-answer style, informal style.

Extended answer questions in exams

Genre – essay

Audience – examiner

Purpose – maximise marks

Style – formal

Learning journal

Genre – journal

Audience – you

Purpose – reflection on learning

Style – informal

Experiment write-up

Genre – science

Audience – teacher

Purpose – to show what you've learned

Style – scientific

This chapter focuses on extended writing, including answers to exam questions.

It's true!

Examiners regularly note in their reports that candidates could improve their answers considerably by ensuring their arguments are clearly laid out and easy to follow.

Objectives

Your learning objectives in this chapter

- Find out why following writing rules makes your writing clearer. Page 61
- Improve your SPaG skills. Page 62
- Use specialist terms to boost your writing and learning. Page 63
- Plan and organise your essay writing. Page 64
- Discover four stages to making points in extended writing. Page 65
- Consider command terms – the words that tell you how to write. Page 66

Now try this

1 Which page of this chapter looks at grammar skills?
2 Which page of this chapter explains 'explain' and evaluates 'evaluate'?

Writing with rules

Whatever genre, style, audience or purpose you are writing for, you will write your best when you are writing about something you are interested in, have strong feelings about or feel connected to. However, there are rules to writing that you need to follow. These rules help you express your meaning clearly and logically and in the appropriate style for your audience.

Read this student's answer to this question: How do study skills help improve essay writing?

Generally speaking, if your writing an essay then study skills are important like time management and planning. its something you have to write in five minites. If you take longer you lose marks Planning is 100% the most important things. My 1 tip is draw a mind map first — all the things you know that connects with it If you are writing with your notes, that is easier but not when you have to remember it all. Then you need memory skills but you needed then earlier!

Now read the feedback the student got from their teacher.

You have covered a very good range of study skills: time management, planning and revision skills. You answered the question directly, well done.
You do need to take more care with your spelling, punctuation and grammar. For example: 'if you're writing an essay', 'It's something you ...' Sometimes you jump from one thing to another. It's not always clear what you mean. Using paragraphs to break up your writing could help with this. Make sure you follow your arguments through and provide evidence to back up your points. For example, why is planning the most important thing? Be specific where you can and avoid vague statements such as 'Generally speaking ...'
I liked your mind map tip — but remember to keep your writing a bit more formal for essays.

Now try this

Write your own answer to the question 'How do study skills help improve essay writing?'. Can you use the teacher's advice to write a better answer than the student did?

SPaG

SPaG stands for Spelling, Punctuation and Grammar and it is a way examiners and teachers give you marks for using good spelling, punctuation and grammar. As you saw on the previous page, shaky SPaG can make written work harder to understand and less convincing.

Extra marks

Some exam questions will have extra marks available for good spelling, punctuation and grammar.

Although you'll be able to see which questions have these marks and which don't, it is a good idea to always aim for good SPaG because it helps you communicate your ideas clearly.

Spelling
Software does a good job of correcting your spelling, but most exams are still handwritten.

1 Check your spelling with an online spelling test (e.g. the Oxford Dictionaries Spelling Challenge).

2 To improve your spelling:
  • get a notebook and keep it with you
  • every time you come across a word you find difficult, write it in your notebook
  • be ambitious – search out hard words
  • test yourself often.

3 Get into online spelling quizzes or hangman or any other game that relies on spelling.

Punctuation
Punctuation is essential in getting your meaning across to a reader. Here are a few pointers.

• Basic level – use full stops at the end of sentences and capital letters to start sentences and for names of people, countries and cities.
• Intermediate level – watch your apostrophes: Simon's cat licks its paws, not Simons cat licks it's paw's.
• Advanced level – read lots of well-edited books and keep a learning eye on the punctuation.

SPaG

Grammar
For your purposes, good grammar is about expressing yourself clearly. Here's one tip:

The most important parts of sentences are the subject, verb and object. The verb is what's being done, the subject is the thing doing it and the object is the thing it is being done to.

Usually, the subject comes first, then the verb, then the object.

Sentences written in that order are usually easy to understand.

Now try this

1 Look back through your work in different subjects and find:
  • three spelling errors
  • three punctuation mistakes.
  Ideally, these would be errors that you've made a few times.

2 Using your study skills knowledge, work out the best way for you to:
  • spell those three words correctly next time you use them
  • turn those three punctuation errors into punctuation triumphs in the future.

Using specialist terms

Your subjects all have specialist terms. Specialist terms are powerful learning tools as they unlock precise meanings. Using them correctly will make your writing clear and specific and will show your audience that you understand your subject.

Where do I find specialist terms?

1 From your teacher. Also, if you have a textbook for your course, there should be a glossary at the back that lists specialist terms for your subject.

2 Next, get a copy of the exam board specification for your course.

3 The specification uses specialist terms to describe what you need to know for each topic. List these terms and use your textbook glossary to add definitions.

4 You could share the work with other students in your group. Setting up a shared document as a *course glossary* would be a great way for you to all work together.

Using specialist terms

Specialist terms are like a magic key – if you use them in the right place and in the right way, you can transform your writing into something remarkable.

Vocabulary building

Learning lists of terms is not the most effective way to boost your specialist vocabulary. Instead, you need to practise using them in context.

Top tip

- For each topic, identify a hit list of specialist terms.
- Every time you see one of your hit list terms in something you are reading, give yourself 5 points.
- Every time you correctly use one of your hit list terms in discussions or in your writing, give yourself 10 points.
- When you've earned 50 points, you have mastered that word and can use it confidently.

Being specific

Vague writing is superficial – just skimming over the surface. Good writing gets stuck in and means what it says.

Here are a few vague sentence starters that you should try to avoid:

- Many experts say ...
- Everyone knows that ...
- Generally speaking, ...

Examiners' report

Examiners look for accurate and relevant use of key terms in written answers. You can often find lists of key terms for each subject in the exam board specification.

Now try this

Pick a textbook for one of your subjects which has a glossary. Starting at the first term under A, see if you can connect that term to the next term in the glossary. Then connect that term to the next one, and so on. What's the longest link of terms you can make? Any connection about the meaning of the terms will do (not just that they start with the same letter!).

Planning extended writing

Many subjects have exam questions involving extended writing – e.g. essay questions. Planning your answer means: 1) you answer the question, 2) you include what you need to and 3) your answer will be clear for other people to understand.

1 Unpicking the question

It is very important to read questions carefully. Students often recognise a specialist term and immediately start writing down everything they know about it. Instead you need to:

STOP + THINK

2 Plan your answer

What does the question want me to do?

The person reading your answer needs to be able to follow your argument.

- Planning your answer means you can set out the steps of your argument first.
- Then you can write your answer so it follows those steps.

It's true!

Examiners consistently report that students who plan their answers well and write a clear response gain more marks than those who do not.

For example, consider this question: Describe and evaluate the advantages of dog ownership for older people. (12 marks)

1 The instruction is to describe and evaluate.
   Plan it: I could do description in one paragraph and evaluation in the next.

2 The topic to cover is: the advantages of dog ownership.
   Plan it: Advantages means more than one – could try for three (?), that makes six paras if I do one description and one evaluation for each advantage.

3 The focus for the topic is: for older people.
   Plan it: what are older people's needs? If I could think of three needs, I could link my evaluations to these three needs …

4 Number of marks = 12.
   Plan it: probably 1 mark for each description and two marks for each evaluation? Time: 5 mins to plan, 15 mins to write maximum.

Plan your time

Top tip

You can usually afford to spend a good five minutes planning an answer to an essay question, depending on how many questions you have to answer in total.

Include time limits in your essay plan. That way you can check that you are on track to finish the question in time.

Here's what the plan might look like written down:

1 State **3** needs of older people.
2 Describe **1st** advantage of dog ownership.
3 Link to **1st** need of older people + evaluate.
4 Describe **2nd** advantage.
5 Link to **2nd** need + evaluate.
6 Describe **3rd** advantage.
7 Link to **3rd** need + evaluate.

Now try this

Find some past papers for a subject you are studying. You can find these by searching online for "past papers" plus the subject and the name of your exam board. Copy out three extended answer questions and write a plan for each based just on what the question asks for.

Making points and backing them up

Paragraphs are the building blocks of extended writing: they help you set out your thoughts clearly so your argument is easy to follow. There's a basic formula to writing an essay / extended answer: make one point per paragraph. But how do you make a point? You've got four main options.

What are your options?

You have different writing options depending on:

- what the question wants from you
- how many marks it is worth
- how much you can remember about it.

Two-stage answers

This is a basic level of answer.

1 State your point.
2 Develop your point.

For example:

1 One disadvantage of owning a dog is having to walk it twice a day.
2 This can be inconvenient if it is raining heavily or, if you go away on holiday, you need to persuade someone else to walk your dog for you.

(You don't need to number points in your actual answer – they are just here for illustration.)

Note that these are only starting points. You would want to create whole paragraphs to support your argument.

Three-stage answers

This is a more advanced answer. You need to be able to remember relevant evidence to back up your point.

1 State your point.
2 Develop your point.
3 Provide evidence / example(s).

For example:

1 Owning a dog can have health benefits for people.
2 People with dogs walk more than people who do not, which means they get more exercise.
3 A survey by Harvard Medical School in 2018 showed that dog ownership was associated with a lower risk of heart disease.

Four-stage answers

This is the best type of answer for use with higher mark questions.

1 State your point.
2 Develop your point.
3 Provide evidence / example(s).
4 Explain what your evidence shows: 'This shows that ...'

The fourth point can also be a second piece of evidence / a second example.

For example:

1 A second advantage of owning a dog is that they provide companionship.
2 Dogs are usually affectionate and loyal and these traits make their owners feel better.
3 Bringing dogs into hospital wards has been shown to improve patients' recovery rates.
4 This evidence shows that the psychological benefits of dog ownership can be very significant.

Now try this

Pick some questions from a past paper for one of your subjects and try writing two-stage, three-stage and four-stage answers. Remember to tackle an extended writing question worth plenty of marks as one of your questions.

Command terms

Command terms are the words in a question that tell you how to write about the topic. For example, describing something is different from comparing it with something else.

Knowledge and understanding

If a question just wants to check you know about something, it will use command terms such as:

- describe
- explain
- list
- outline
- name
- what is meant by ...?

Application

Questions that ask you to show you know how to make your knowledge work for you will use command terms such as:

- calculate
- examine
- show how ...
- using an example
- using your knowledge of ...
- explain.

Analysis

Analysis means breaking things down so you can see how something all works together. Command terms include:

- analyse
- compare / contrast
- discuss
- examine
- explain
- identify.

Analysis and evaluation often involve comparing advantages and disadvantages or similarities and differences. Keep your answer balanced. That means that you cover a similar number of points for the two aspects.

Evaluation

Evaluation means 'to assess the value of something'. Command terms include:

- assess
- consider
- evaluate
- explain why
- to what extent ...
- how far do you agree that ...?

Evaluation questions usually have the highest number of marks because they are the most difficult.

Golden rules for writing

- Extended writing questions can sometimes combine different terms, e.g. 'Define and explain ...' or 'Using examples, evaluate ...'
- If a question asks for an example, it needs to be one that is relevant to the question.
- Adding detail to develop your points is a great way to add marks for all these different types of question.
- One point per paragraph is a useful rule for writing. This makes it easier for your reader to understand your arguments.
- Use 'lead in' sentences to start paragraphs too. These can flag up to the reader what you are doing. For example: 'Another disadvantage of ...'

Now try this

1 If any of your courses use case studies or other types of named example, make a list of all the studies and examples you need to know for the topics you are studying. You can find this information in the specifications for your courses – make sure you get the right exam board for each.

2 Practise writing about these examples. Maybe you could check some past papers and find three different places where you need to use a named example?

The writing challenge

Here are the writing challenge tasks for your progress tracker. **Page 97**

1 Use a dictionary to find ten words you didn't know before. Write them down plus their meanings.

Use three of them (correctly) in conversation or in your writing.

Use this space to record the three words you used.

1

2

3

Well done.
Add a tick to your progress tracker. ●

2 Put together a hit list of specialist **Page 63** terms.

When you have ten terms you have completed the challenge.

Use this space to record your ten specialist terms. Make sure you understand what they mean and how to use them!

Well done. Add a tick to your progress tracker. ●

3 Look through your answers to extended essay questions that you've done in class.

Pick one – ideally, one that you think could have gone better.

Use what you've learned in this chapter to identify how you could have improved your answer.

Use this space to record the areas for improvement you identified. You can use this knowledge to improve your next essay.

Well done. Add a tick to your progress tracker. ●

Quick quiz

1 What does SPaG stand for?
2 Outline the advantages of dog ownership.

Points to remember: writing

You are often asked to write things to demonstrate how much you have learned about a topic and whether you can apply what you've learned in different ways.

1 Writing is a very important part of learning because you bring together what you've learned and make it your own.

That's why academic honesty is so important. If you copy someone else's writing, you are not learning effectively.
 Page 56

Top tip

2 There are many different types of learning. For every type, think of GAPS: genre, audience, purpose and style.

Purpose is particularly important for learning. Find a purpose to your writing that interests you. That will help you learn more and feel more motivated.

 Top tip

3 Although writing should be your chance to express yourself, you have to make your meaning clear to your audience.

Your writing should follow the rules for SPaG and be well organised. Planning how your writing is organised will help readers follow your argument.

Top tip

4 Specialist terms are like magic keys to learning about a subject.

If you build up your knowledge of specialist terms for your subjects, and use them correctly in your writing, you will be able to demonstrate a deeper understanding of topics that will help you do well in your studies.

Top tip

Now try this

Command terms are used in exam questions to tell you what to do. Can you match each command term to the correct description of what you need to do if you see one?

(Command terms may be slightly different for different exam boards and different subjects.)

1 Describe	a	Plan out a general **overview** of something: give the key points but don't go into detail.
2 Outline	b	Work out the **value** of something by weighing up its strengths and its limitations.
3 Examine	c	Set out a detailed account that includes **reasons** and causes.
4 Explain	d	Identify the **similarities** and **differences** between two (or more) things in a balanced way.
5 Compare	e	**Unpick** the way something works: uncover the assumptions that hold it together and the way one part links with another part.
6 Identify	f	Give a detailed **account** of something.
7 Evaluate	g	**Pick out** one explanation from a selection of different options.

Importance of memory skills

When it is possible to search for any information online, why do we still need to memorise information? One good reason is that you need to remember a lot of information for your exams. Here are four memorable things about the way your brain remembers things.

Did you know ...?

Your brain loves things to be organised into groups and categories because that helps it to attach meaning to things.

Your brain loves stories. One way to help your brain remember things is to connect them to a narrative – make a story out of them.

Your brain looks for differences, things that look out of place – especially odd combinations of things. They are much more memorable.

Your brain will remember more when you revise actively – make your own notes, concept maps, flashcards, etc., rather than using someone else's.

It's true!

In the classroom, scientists have found that the more ways something is introduced to the brain and reviewed, the more regions of the brain will store that information. This will form connections and these multiple stimulations to the brain will mean better memory.

Page 35

Objectives

Your learning objectives in this chapter

- Find out what mnemonics are and how they work.   Page 70

- Try out three mnemonic techniques for yourself.   Pages 71, 72 and 73

- Discover how concept maps can help with making memory connections.   Page 74

- Reconnect with study skills from the rest of this book that can help make things memorable.   Page 75

Now try this

1 Which page(s) of this chapter gives you some memory techniques to try out?

2 Which page of this chapter makes links to things you've already learned in this book?

Mnemonics

People use a lot of different techniques to remember things. Sometimes these are called mnemonics (pronounced 'nu-monics'). This page summarises some different approaches. We will then go on to look at three mnemonic techniques in more detail.

First-letter mnemonics

This technique uses a phrase to help you remember the first letters of a sequence of key words.

For example, Richard Of York Gave Battle In Vain for the colours of the spectrum in the correct order, namely: Red, Orange, Yellow, Green, Blue, Indigo, Violet.

It's true!

Researchers found that many students using mnemonics substantially out-performed those who did not.

Try them out – they may work for you!

Using pictures

Connecting words with an image often helps to make the words easier to remember – your brain uses the image memory to prompt the word memory.

This technique is often used with flashcards, for example when learning words in another language. Page 85

Using different senses

Some people remember their PINs because of the shape the numbers make. Other people remember things better if they hear them rather than read them. Page 35

Making something look odd

Making something look odd so it stands out from everything around it is a really good way of getting your brain to pay attention. There's more on this on the next page.

Meaningful memories

Research shows that it is a lot easier to remember things that are meaningful to you, that you find interesting or relevant. Setting learning goals, asking questions, putting things into your own words and reflecting on your learning can help to make what you study more memorable.

Making connections

Research also shows that making connections between what you are learning now and what you have learned before makes memories stronger. The more you make these connections, the easier it should become to recall the information you need in a test or an exam.

Now try this

1 What can you remember about your most recent school lesson?
   How do you retrieve your memories? For example, do you see them like a film? Is there audio?

2 Identify any strategies shown on this page that you think might help you get more detail from your memories.

Weird pairs

Your brain likes to make connections and picks up on unusual things. This mnemonic technique uses both these facts to help you learn lists of things in order.

Have a look at the list of words opposite. The weird pairs technique will enable you to:

- remember all of them
- remember them in the same order
- remember them so well that you could list them backwards.

You need to put in a little time to get the results, but it is a very powerful way of getting information into your long-term memory.

1	scout	11	mob
2	lunch	12	prison
3	tyre	13	balcony
4	trousers	14	court
5	watch	15	tea
6	soap	16	escape
7	church	17	Halloween
8	sister	18	ham
9	rabid	19	knife
10	rifle	20	boo

How the weird pairs technique works

Top tip

You link the first two words on the list in some memorable way. For example, here are scouts having lunch.

Then you link the second word with the third word – for example, this woman is tucking into a tasty lunch of tyre. The weirder the link, the easier it will be to remember.

And so on – so the next link is tyre-trousers.

This technique might seem to be taking a while at first, but it is something you get quicker at with practice.

Try it out

1. Now make your own connection between the first word and the word after it. This connection:
   - should be weird – the more unusual and funny the better
   - should have the two things interacting in some way, rather than just being next to each other.
2. Spend a little time thinking about the image. If it is funny, let yourself feel amused. If it is revolting, feel that emotion too.
3. Now do the same for the second word in the list and the word after that.
4. Continue to link one word to the next until you get to the end.

Now try this

1. Once you have gone through the list, making your weird interactions between each word, close this page and see how many you can remember.
2. Can you recite the list backwards?
3. Can you still recite it this time tomorrow? (You'll have to wait a bit to answer this one.)

If you have studied *To Kill A Mockingbird* in English Literature, you'll have recognised that the words in the list are connected to the main events, in order, of that novel's plotline.

Number pairs

This mnemonic system is similar to the weird pairs technique. It involves using numbers and you can use it to help remember which number something is on a list or in a sequence.

The number pairs system is like the weird pairs technique (see previous page) except that you use numbers instead of links between each pair.

Numbers aren't very easy to make strong visual links to, so the number pairs system converts them into words.

The list opposite uses words that rhyme with numbers.

Top tip

1 = Bun	
2 = Shoe	
3 = Tree	
4 = Door	
5 = Hive	
6 = Sticks	
7 = Heaven	
8 = Plate	
9 = Line	
10 = Hen	

Try it out

Using number pairs

GCSE History specifications often require students to understand the ways the Nazis used propaganda to control and influence attitudes in 1933–39. Here are five things you might remember:

1 Nazis took control of the media, including all radio broadcasts.

2 They used films and posters to spread propaganda messages.

3 They organised rallies – huge spectacles of support for the regime.

4 They used the 1936 Berlin Olympics for international propaganda.

5 All writers, artists, journalists and musicians had to register with the Ministry of Public Enlightenment and Propaganda to get their work approved.

You then combine the number rhymes with the things on the list, as with weird pairs. For example:

1 Number one is **bun** so pair one from the list could be a bun squashing a radio (because number 1 on the list above is bun).

2 Number two is **shoe** so pair two from the list could be a film projector showing **shoes** marching.

3 Number three is **tree** so pair three from the list could be a Nazi rally with every supporter holding a **tree**.

Come up with your own pairs for numbers four and five – you don't need to draw them; the drawings here are just to give you the idea.

Now try this

1 Write a list of ten items and use the number pairs system to remember it by number.

2 One advantage of the number pairs system is that you have to make fewer links. How does it compare with the weird pairs technique for you – which one do you prefer and why?

The journey technique

One possible problem with the weird pairs technique is that if you forget one connection, the link in the whole chain gets broken. The journey technique gets round that in a clever way.

For this technique you need a journey you know very well, for example your trip to school.

Take that trip in your mind right now. Take note of points along the route that stand out for you: a bus stop, perhaps, or a shop or a friend's house.

You use this familiar journey and these points to help you remember things in order.

- As with the weird pairs, you think of a strong visual image for each thing on your list. Page 71

- 'Stick' the image for the first thing on your list onto the first point on your route.

- Do the same for everything on your list – each item on the list gets stuck onto a point on your route.

- Review the journey when you need to remember the list of things!

The memory palace

Top tip

You can also use the journey technique without mentally leaving your house.

Imagine a trip through your front door, into the hall, along to the kitchen ... Note things along the way you could use to stick your list items onto.

It's true!

Memory experts can even create whole memory palaces made of imaginary rooms, and mentally walk around them to retrieve vast amounts of stored data.

Try creating a memory palace for yourself starting in your bedroom.

This girl has used objects in her bedroom to help her remember the electro-magnetic spectrum.

Radio waves
Microwaves
Infra-red
Light waves
Ultra-violet
Gamma   X-rays

The electromagnetic spectrum goes: radio waves, microwaves, infra-red, light waves, ultra-violet radiation, X-rays and gamma radiation.

Examiners' report

"Knowledge of times tables and the ability to multiply and divide effectively were often disappointing and led to a loss of marks."

Learning some things by heart – the electromagnetic spectrum, times tables or other facts and figures – can make tricky questions easier.

Now try this

Try the journey technique out for yourself. Which works better for you – a journey you know well or a trip around your home?

Maps for memories

Concept maps are a great way to develop ideas – and they also help you remember the connections between ideas.

Page 37

Top tip

Memories get strengthened the more times you make connections to them.

That makes a concept map a very good tool for building up memories and for recalling memories when you need them.

You can build up a concept map of a topic in three main stages.

1 Identify what you already know about a new topic as you begin learning about it.

> Use a big piece of paper (A3) or do it on a computer so there's plenty of room to expand your map.

2 As you work through your topic, add new connections to your concept map. This could be a good thing to do as part of your reflection on the topic.

> You could also leave this until right at the end of the topic when you can look back over everything you've learned.

3 When you are revising this topic for a test or an exam, your concept map will show you what you need to cover and how it all connects.

> A good revision strategy is to see if you can redraw your topic concept map from memory.

Here's an example of how a concept map could develop as a student worked through the Religious Studies topic of 'Christian beliefs about life after death'.

First, the student maps what they already know about this topic:

As they go through the topic, the student adds more connections and updates previous ones:

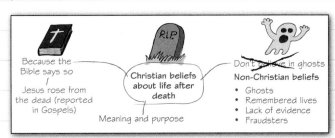

By the end of the topic, the concept map shows everything the student covered in that topic:

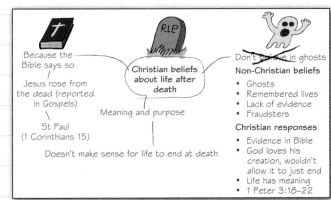

Now try this

Try out this method of concept mapping a topic for yourself. How could you refine it to make your concept map connections more memorable?

Making memory connections

Many of the study skills in this book also help with remembering what you have learned. Look up the page, read the information and write in your own connections to how each skill could help build up effective memories.

Setting goals and objectives

Describe how setting a learning goal for a topic could help you remember more about it.

Page 12

Explain why the productive chunking technique of avoiding interruptions could help make topics more memorable.

Page 30

Hint: setting goals for topics makes them more interesting and relevant to you.

Hint: this technique helps you focus your attention.

15 minutes
15 minutes   15 minutes
15 minutes

Learning approaches

Why might switching your revision approach make a topic stick in your memory a bit more?

Page 35

In what ways could the SQ3R reading method build stronger memories to your reading and notes?

Pages 54 and 55

Hint: remember that your brain looks out for unusual things and differences.

Hint: putting things into your own words activates important parts of your brain.

Adding challenges and rewards

Why might adding challenges and rewards to your learning help you remember more?

Page 10

Hint: it is often harder to remember things that you find boring or unpleasant.

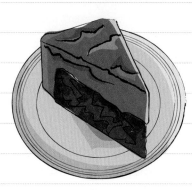

Now try this

Online memory tests are a fun way to help you understand how your memory works. Understanding your memory will enable you to build up your memory skills.

The face memory test is a good place to start: search for "Face memory test".

A lot of people are surprised at what their memory can do when faces are involved. Were you?

The memory challenge

Here are the memory challenges for your progress tracker. Page 97

1 Use one of the memory techniques in this chapter to memorise the first ten elements of the periodic table:

1) Hydrogen, 2) Helium, 3) Lithium, 4) Beryllium, 5) Boron, 6) Carbon, 7) Nitrogen, 8) Oxygen, 9) Fluorine, 10) Neon.

You can use what they sound like as well as the whole word. For example, Boron might make you think of Boring.

Cover up the list of the first ten elements and, using just your memory, write down here which elements are at numbers:

4)

7)

9)

Well done.
Add a tick to your progress tracker.

2 For the next new topic you start, develop a concept map, starting with what you already know about the topic and adding new connections as you cover them (or at the end of the topic when you review what you've learned).

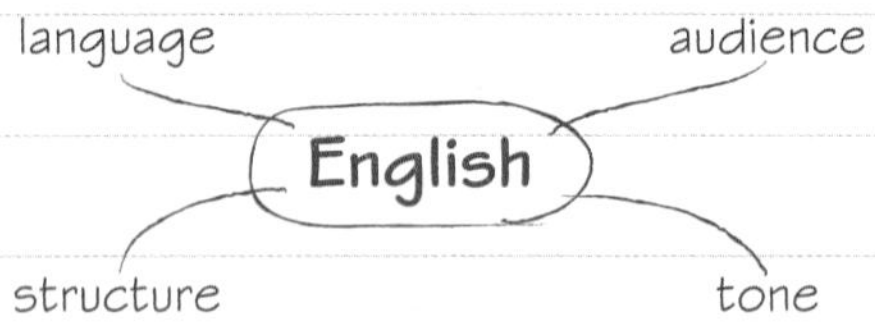
language
audience
English
structure
tone

Note here:

- the topic you chose
- a brief description of the concept map
- where you put it so that you can find it when you want to review what you've learned.

Well done.
Add a tick to your progress tracker.

3 Flick through your notes for all your subjects for last term.

How many pages looked:

- very familiar
- vaguely familiar
- like you'd never seen them before?

Reflect on the following questions.

1 What did the very familiar pages have in common, if anything?

2 What did the unfamiliar pages have in common, if anything?

Of your flick-through audit, how many pages were:

very familiar	
vaguely familiar	
like you'd never seen them before?	

Record here your conclusions from the two reflection questions.

Well done.
Add a tick to your progress tracker.

Quick quiz

1 What page in this chapter connects memory with mockingbirds?

2 What page mentions trousers?

Points to remember: remembering

Exams involve a lot of remembering: the good news is that when you learn effectively, you are already building up the strong memory connections that will help you recall what you need when you need it.

1 Human evolution has hard-wired your brain to find some things more memorable than others.

You can work with your brain to process information in the right way to make it most memorable. For example, using stories, categories or differences.

2 All the things that make learning effective also make what you are learning easier to remember.

If you put your study skills into action throughout your course, you will find revision easier. Make connections, find what interests you about a topic and review your learning.

3 Memory techniques often depend on making unusual connections between things.

You can use unusual connections to remember anything from your subjects. It takes a bit of effort, but there is potentially a big reward.

4 If you think that you haven't got a very good memory, you are almost certainly wrong.

Humans have evolved amazing memories and we all have them. The trick is to find the right way to get yours working for you.

Now try this

This student has a memory challenge for you.

> Can you memorise the kings and queens of Britain from 1707 to the date this book was published – in the right order? That's Anne, George I, George II, George III, George IV, William IV, Victoria, Edward VII, George V, Edward VIII, George VI, Elizabeth II.

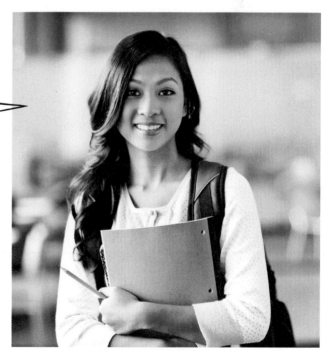

Will you accept the challenge? It's information that is bound to come in useful some day. If you do, what memory technique would you use to help you?

Planning your revision

Like every other kind of study, you will feel much more in control of revising for exams if you plan your revision and decide which strategies to use to make it as effective as possible.

Five reasons to think positively about exams

1 Everything you learn in your courses can help you in your exams.

2 Exams are a great opportunity to show what you can do. Potentially, good exam results could unlock some really exciting doors in your life.

3 The people who are marking your exam paper *want* to give you all the marks they can.

4 Your teachers are exam experts. You have access to all their expertise to help you do your best.

5 Preparing for exams gives you experience of building up to a big challenge. This is useful experience for whatever you go on to do after school.

I know this.

Planning ahead

Everyone is at least a little bit nervous about exams. You can use that nervous energy to get lots done, but it can also make it harder to think coolly and calmly about how to do your revision.

That is why it makes a lot of sense to plan out your revision well in advance of your exams. Your teachers will let you know when to start.

Objectives

Your learning objectives in this chapter

- Explore some revision strategies recommended by other students.   Page 79

- Understand how to plan your revision and create exam checklists.   Pages 80, 81, 82 and 83

- Evaluate three specific revision skills.   Pages 84, 85 and 86

- Investigate past papers and keeping answers relevant to the question.   Pages 87 and 88

- Consider how study skills can help reduce study-related stress.   Page 89

It's true!

Studies have found that certain learning techniques can really help students perform better. You just need to find which techniques work for you.

Now try this

1 Which page of this chapter takes advice from other students?

2 Which page of this chapter looks at stress?

Revision strategies

Here are some student recommendations on revision strategies that worked for them.
In the following four pages, we will look at some of these strategies in more detail.

It worked best for me to do three 15-minute chunks of revision on one subject, have a break and then do my next block of revision on a new subject.

I made summary notes in the build-up to the exams. Right before the exams I didn't try to learn anything new – I made summary notes of my summary notes!

It really helped to revise with someone so we could test each other.

And being able to compare our notes really helped us understand some topics.

I turned my notes into flashcards and I also wrote key words on Post-Its and stuck them up all over the house!

We recorded study notes and played them on the bus to college.

It was an idea we got from finding out about the auditory learning style.

I used past exam papers and wrote answers to the questions. Writing down what I knew, using it to answer exam questions – that really worked for me.

Now try this

There are lots of revision tips online, covering a wide range of different levels of study. Search for ones specific to GCSE and put together a list of your top five. Include notes to remind yourself why you thought each of the five looked as if it would work well for you.

Revision planning

Planning your revision will help you to use your time productively, ensure you cover what you need to and help you identify where you need to put in the most effort.

1 Find out when your exams are for each subject.

Your teachers will tell you these dates – and any others you need to know.

2 Work out how much time there is between the date you plan to start revising and when your exams start. Start revising as early as you can.

Put these dates in your planner. Closer to the actual exams, **double-check** the date, time and location of each exam so you are 100% certain where you need to be and at what time.

There are usually different exam papers for different units of your course, so you will have more than one exam per subject.

- Block out times when you know you are busy doing something else.
- Decide how many hours a day you can revise for. Be realistic – you need a balance of revision, leisure and rest.

Once you've got a rough idea of how much revision time you have in total (your time bank), divide it by the number of exams you have.

3 Prioritise your exam list in terms of revision time required.

- Which subject and paper is the most important?
- Which needs the most revision?
- Often subjects you find harder need a bit more revision time than subjects you find easier.

4 Allocate each exam paper its own revision time allowance from your total time bank.

5 Now work out your revision blocks.

- You will want to be revising for each paper the day before you take that exam, so put your first revision block for that paper on that day.
- Do the same for all your exams. Then work backwards in time, giving each exam a block here and a block there until you've spent all the time allocations for each exam paper.

REVISE GCSE
REVISION PLANNER

Following your plan

Stick to your plan as much as you can. It might be tempting to stay with one subject if you get into it, but your brain will appreciate a break and a change of scene.

Don't get distracted by creating a beautiful revision plan or researching different apps to help you plan. Make it quickly, and simply get revising! You can also buy planners that are all ready to go.

Now try this

1 Find out the dates of your exams and put them all into your planner.

2 There are a couple of examples of revision planning opposite – study them and then have a go at planning your revision. When are you going to start revising? How much time a day will you spend on revision? How long will your revision chunks be?

Revision planning

Find out your exam dates and write them in your school planner.

- Make sure you know the times of each exam.

- Your teacher will also tell you which rooms the exams will be in – write that information down too.

- You now know how many exams you have and when and where they are. This information will help you plan your revision.

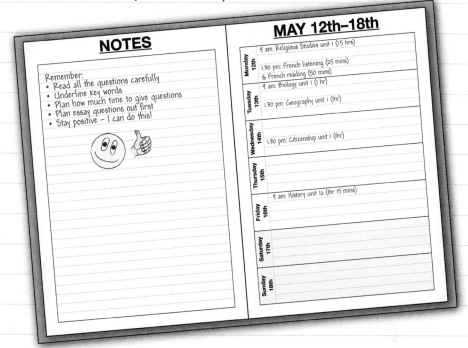

NOTES

Remember:
- Read all the questions carefully
- Underline key words
- Plan how much time to give questions
- Plan essay questions out first
- Stay positive – I can do this!

MAY 12th–18th

Monday 12th	9 am: Religious Studies unit 1 (1.5 hrs)
	1.30 pm: French listening (25 mins) & French reading (50 mins)
Tuesday 13th	9 am: Biology unit 1 (1 hr)
	1.30 pm: Geography unit 1 (1hr)
Wednesday 14th	1.30 pm: Citizenship unit 1 (1hr)
Thursday 15th	
Friday 16th	9 am: History unit 1a (1hr 15 mins)
Saturday 17th	
Sunday 18th	

Filling in your planner

Work out when you can revise and what your revision blocks are going to be.

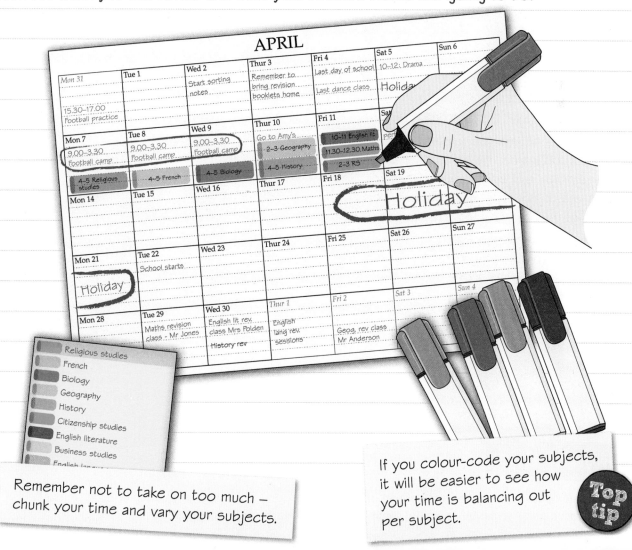

Remember not to take on too much – chunk your time and vary your subjects.

Top tip

If you colour-code your subjects, it will be easier to see how your time is balancing out per subject.

81

Revision planning: exam checklist

As well as working out when you will be revising which subjects, it is also a good idea to create a checklist of what you need to cover for each exam you are taking. There are two main types of information you need for your exam checklist.

1 What you need to cover for the exam – the topics

The very best place to check what you need to cover is the specification for each subject.

You can download these from the exam board websites, but it is best to get this information from your teacher because:

- you have to know which exam board you are following
- there are sometimes different versions of specifications for different years
- if the specification has options, you need to know which options you are doing.

2 Information about the exam
This could include:

- date of exam
- time of exam and duration
- location (which room)
- how many questions to answer
- what you are allowed to take into the exam with you, e.g. dictionaries, calculators.

It's true!

These instructions may seem obvious, but examiners say it is not unusual for students to turn up at the wrong time, on the wrong day or even to the wrong place.

Your Pearson Revision Guides will help you know which topics to cover!

Key exam information

Your teachers will let you know the information on dates, times and locations of your exams, and everything you need to know about how the exam papers work.

If you want to go over the information about the exam papers again for a subject, ask your teacher for a recent past exam paper. The front cover always contains instructions.

Your surname, followed by other names

Your school's exam number goes here

How long the exam lasts

Your personal exam number. Your teacher will give you this

Which questions, if any, have marks for SPaG

How many questions to tackle (it may be all of them or only some)

Remember: most subjects you take will have more than one exam paper – unit 1, unit 2, etc.

All exam papers are different and liable to change. This is an example of the key information you may find on your paper.

Now try this

The page opposite has an example of part of an exam checklist. Have a go at creating one for yourself – you'll need to ask a teacher to supply some of the information you'll need.

Revision planning: exam checklist

Exam checklist

Example

Exam title: Edexcel History: Option 11: Medicine in Britain / Western Front
Time and date of exam: 9am, Friday 16 May.
Length of exam: 1 hour 15 mins.　　　　　　　　　　Room: School hall.

Answer questions: 1 and 2 from Section A, then 3 and 4 from Section B and either 5 or 6.

Topics to cover	Had a go	Nearly there	Nailed it!
c.1250–c.1500: Medieval medicine			
Supernatural and religious ideas about disease	✓	✓	✓
Galen – Four Humours and miasma	✓	✓	
Treatment: religious, bloodletting, purifying air, etc.			
Black Death case study	✓	✓	✓
c.1500–c.1700: Medical Renaissance			
Continuity: Galen's influence and church influence	✓	✓	
Change: scientific approach: Thomas Sydenham			
Change: communication from printing press and Royal Society	✓		
Continuity: treatment, e.g. hospitals			
Change: treatment: Vesalius' influence	✓	✓	✓
Case study: William Harvey and circulation of blood			
Case study: Great Plague, London, 1665			
c.1700–c.1900: 18th and 19th C			
Change: germ theory: Pasteur and Koch on microbes	✓		
Change: better training and hospitals: Florence Nightingale	✓	✓	
Change: anaesthetics and antiseptics			
Change & prevention: vaccinations	✓	✓	
Change & prevention: Public Health Act 1875			
Case study: Jenner and vaccination			
Case study: Cholera and John Snow, 1854	✓	✓	
c.1900 to present day			
Change: genetics and lifestyle factors	✓	✓	
Change: blood tests, scans, monitors	✓		
Change: NHS and advances in treatment	✓	✓	
Change & prevention: mass vaccinations			
Change & prevention: government, lifestyle campaigns			
Case study: Fleming, Florey & Chain			
Case study: fight against lung cancer			

Condensing your notes and handouts

Your notes and handouts are a very important revision resource because they link you directly to what you have learned in class. Condensing these notes makes revision more manageable.

1 Organise

The first step is to get all your notes and handouts together and organised into subjects and topics.

Top tip Check for any gaps in your notes – the easiest way to do this is to compare what you have for each subject with a friend doing the same subject.

2 Summarise

For each page of notes, write a summary of the main points onto a piece of A4 paper.

Top tip

If you check your notes against a textbook and there seems like a lot you haven't covered, check with your teacher before you start trying to learn a lot of new material.

If you've made your notes using methods from earlier, you'll already have a summary to work from. **Pages 44 and 45**

3 Condense

Now condense each summary down to the main ideas, key terms and key points.

Write your condensed notes onto index cards, leaving plenty of space between points.

Condensed notes are easier to revise from and the process of condensing your notes also helps you remember your topics.

Now try this

Practise summarising and condensing three notes from three of your subjects. If you find it difficult to know what to leave out, try highlighting key points in your notes or concept mapping your notes first to identify the most important parts.

Page 37

Page 74

Flashcards

Once you have condensed your notes, you may find flashcards work well for you as a way of revising key terms and concepts.

Flashcards work in a really simple way.

- On one side of a card, write something you need to know.
- On the other side of the card, write the answer.

The big advantage of flashcards is that you are revising while you make them, and then you can test yourself or get someone else to test you.

It's true!

Recent research has found that flashcards are one of the most effective techniques for retaining information.

> Words to use for writing about poetry 1
>
> ## Assonance

> Words to use for writing about poetry
>
> Assonance =
> when vowel sounds are repeated
>
> E.g. "And the Raven, never flitting, still is sitting, still is sitting ..."
> – Edgar Allen Poe, *The Raven*

Making flashcards

You can make flashcards:

- using index cards or a sheet of card cut into A6-sized pieces
- using Post-Its – stick them around your room for a ready-made memory journey
- using PowerPoint – the first slide of each pair is the question and the second is the answer.

Top tip

Flashcards work well for:

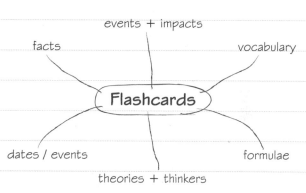

facts
events + impacts
vocabulary
Flashcards
dates / events
theories + thinkers
formulae

Digital flashcards

There are also other people's flashcards online – these can be good for a test but it is better to make your own because you learn more that way.

Smartphone flashcard apps can be fun – but be careful not to waste time on flashcards that don't match your GCSE exam.

Other techniques

Flashcards are not so useful for revising processes or skills, or applying your knowledge and understanding in different ways.

- Flow charts, timelines and diagrams can help with revising processes. *Page 86*
- Practising exam questions with past papers is the key to using skills and applying what you've learned. *Page 88*

Now try this

Create a deck of flashcards for a topic from one of your GCSE subjects.

Flow diagrams

Flow diagrams work well for revising processes and sequences, for example remembering the steps in an experiment in Science or, for History, the sequence of events leading to the Nazis' 1933 election victory.

Here is a flow diagram for using a light microscope safely. To use a microscope, you need to follow a specific sequence of steps.

Start with the lowest power objective under the eyepiece.

↓

Clip the slide securely on the stage.

↓

Adjust the light source (mirror) so that light goes up through the slide.

↓

Use the coarse focusing wheel to focus on the slide.

↓

Move the slide so that the object you need is in the middle of the view.

↓

If needed, move a higher power objective into position above the slide.

↓

Use the **fine focusing wheel** to bring the cell back into focus.

Using a microscope safely is important for investigating biological specimens.

Read this GCSE Geography text extract and, in the space underneath it, draw your own flow chart to summarise the process it describes.

In the remote countryside the process of rural–urban migration causes the countryside to lose population, particularly young people of working age. People become dissatisfied with the quality of life and lack of services, and leave for better opportunities elsewhere. The problem is that when young people leave, the demand for local services falls. This means that shops and other services close. Schools close because there aren't enough children. The loss of services makes the area even less attractive and more people choose to leave.

Draw your flow diagram of the process here:

Now try this

1   Come up with three processes from your subjects then summarise them with a flow chart.
2   A timeline is a sort of flow diagram that uses dates instead of boxes. What could you use a timeline for in your revision?

Revising with past papers

Past papers are exam papers from previous years. Most revision experts would agree that practising exam questions is the very best way to revise for GCSE exams, because it means you have to apply what you've learned in different scenarios.

There are two parts to past papers and you need both.

1 The question paper – this will be just like your real exam paper in style and layout.

2 The mark scheme – this is the answer sheet for the question paper. Examiners use mark schemes to decide how many marks to give answers.

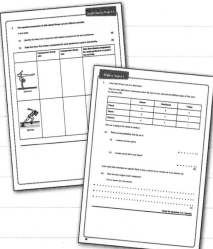

Mark schemes for extended answer questions can be quite difficult to interpret. Your teacher will explain how they work and this will give you an excellent insight into how to access your best marks for these questions.

Examiners' report

"Use the number of marks available for each question as an indication of how long you should spend answering each question."

Look at the number of marks as a guide to how much you should write.

How to revise with past papers

1 Work through the past paper under timed conditions.

2 Do every question as in your real exam.

3 Do not stop to look something up in a textbook or your notes.

4 When you have finished, check your answers with the mark scheme.

5 Use your results to diagnose areas where you need more revision.

6 Go back to your notes and textbook to improve each answer.

Past papers can't help you predict what questions will come up for your exam, so don't just revise the topics you see on one or two old exam papers.

Top tip

If you see questions that just don't make any sense to you, don't just skip them and look for something easier. Use past papers to identify gaps in your understanding – then plug those gaps with revision.

Now try this

Search for a past paper for one of your subjects.

1 Pick a high marks question and spend ten minutes brainstorming an answer to it – you don't need to write the answer itself, just plan out how you would tackle it.

2 For each topic you revise, practise thinking up questions an examiner could ask you about it. Use the command terms to help you.

Page 66

Practising exam questions

The key thing to remember whenever you answer exam questions is to keep everything relevant to the question. This applies as much when you are practising your answers in revision as when you are answering them for real in your exams.

Keep your answer relevant

When you recognise a topic in an exam question, and you can remember something about it, it is really tempting to write down everything you can remember.

However, this is the wrong approach. You need to take a moment and think about the question. What is it asking you to do? What information do you have that is relevant?

Hi, I'm an examiner. I can only reward you for points that are **relevant** to the exam question.

Knowledge of the specification can help you with your revision and exams.

How do you know what's relevant?

It helps to know that exam questions for a subject are closely related to the exam specification for that subject.

If your revision can make the same connections within topics as the specification does, then it is easier to decide what is relevant to the question and what is not.

If you follow the instructions for creating an exam checklist you will see these connections every time you use your checklists.   **Pages 82 and 83**

Examiners' report

"Candidates must be guided and advised to write in the space provided."
Don't assume that writing very long answers will necessarily result in a better score. Excellent answers may be concise.

How much to write?

Find out how much to include by seeing how many marks are available.

Every point you make should be geared towards answering the question. If a point isn't helping, it is not relevant.

Top tip

When looking at an exam specification:
- be aware that each section is about something **specific**
- look for **command terms**
- notice that it includes **specialist terms**.

Now try this

Look at the sample exam checklist. If an exam question asked you to give one example of continuity and one example of change in the period c.1250–c.1700, what would your answer be?   **Page 83**

Dealing with stress

Some people find stress helpful; some find it very unhelpful. Thinking positively about ways to make stress work for you isn't strictly a study skill, but study skills can help with reducing stress, both in the run-up to exams and all the way through school. Here are some common factors that add to stress.

Your lifestyle

late nights / not enough sleep

earning money — Lifestyle — junk food

too many commitments

Your relationships

peer pressure

nowhere quiet to study at home

issues with boyfriend / girlfriend

Relationships

pressure from parent(s)

fall-outs with friends

Organisation

missing deadlines

procrastination

Organisation

late with homework / coursework

not leaving enough time for revision

Revision methods

'cramming' – too much too late

reading notes without taking it in

Revision

social media distractions

no revision timetable

not revising

revising without breaks

Positive actions

That's enough of the negatives – here are some positive points to help you take control of your revision and reduce unhelpful stress.

Try to have a healthy lifestyle. Eat well and get plenty of sleep.

Remember the SQ3R method? It's a great way to revise effectively: it gives a focus to your notes and engages your brain in making sense of what you are reading. **Page 54**

Take control of your revision. Decide what you want to achieve and set revision objectives and goals. Reward yourself for achieving them.

The productive chunking technique is a great way to protect your time from distractions and you get a sense of achievement for each 15-minute chunk you complete. **Page 30**

Talk to friends and family about what you need to do well in exams. If you can't find a quiet place to study, talk to a teacher.

Now try this

If you do find yourself getting stressed by exams, try controlled breathing. Breathe slowly in and out, with one hand on your stomach. Try to make your stomach push out as you breathe in, and pull in as you breathe out. Just focus on your breathing, until you start to feel a bit calmer.

The revising challenge

Here are the revising challenges for your progress tracker. ▸ Page 97

1 Find out when your exams are. You can ask your teachers or you can check online (if you know which exam board you are studying) for next year's exam times.

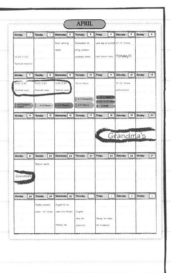

How many exams do you have in total?

When is your first exam and what is it?

When is your last exam and what is it?

Well done.
Add a tick to your progress tracker. ●

2 Complete an exam checklist for one exam from one subject.

You may need to ask your teacher for the content requirements from the subject's specification. You can search for the specification yourself if you know the exam board and the year you'll be taking your exam.

What are the three topics for this exam that you are most looking forward to revising?

1
2
3

What are the three topics from this exam that you think you'll need to spend the most time revising?

1
2
3

Well done.
Add a tick to your progress tracker. ●

3 Reflect on the revision you have done in the past – for tests and mock exams. What techniques have you found useful? What has not worked so well for you? What are the obstacles or difficulties you face when it comes to revision? And what will you do differently next time you revise?

Record here your conclusions about what you will do differently next time you revise.

Well done.
Add a tick to your progress tracker. ●

Quick quiz

1 What is assonance?
2 Which king came after George V?

Points to remember: revising

In some ways, revision skills are a condensed form of the study skills you've covered in the rest of this book: organisation and time management for your revision planner, learning to learn strategies and skills, with notes for revision strategies and writing skills for answering questions.

With luck, the study skills in this book will also help a bit with feeling more in control and dealing with exam stress.

So the points to remember here are relevant for this chapter, but also for the book as a whole.

1 When there is only a limited amount of time and a lot to do, being organised and managing your time means you can work efficiently and effectively.

Planning your study time and your revision time is your foundation for study success.

Top tip

2 Setting goals for your learning is the framework for your study success. Only you can say how far you want to go with your studies and how high you will reach.

Remember that objectives are your steps up to achieving your goals; and every step deserves a little reward.

Top tip

3 Thinking about your learning is the most advanced study skill there is. Knowing what works for you, which techniques to use, how things connect means you can design the way you learn to suit your needs.

Take the time to review what you have put together with these skills and they'll just get better and better.

Top tip

4 Motivation is what drives you to improve and it is the cement that lets you build one block of learning on top of another.

Motivation is often strongest when you feel most in control of what you are doing: when you have set the goals, when you are asking the questions and finding the answers.

Top tip

Learning pyramid

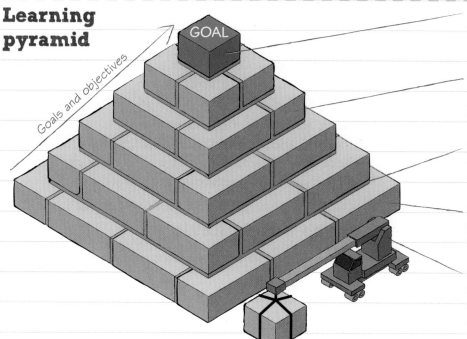

Goals and objectives

GOAL

All these study skills will help you achieve your **GOAL**

Objectives are the building blocks that help you reach your goal

Motivation is the cement that lets you build one block of learning on top of another

Organisation and **time management** are the foundations for your learning

Learning skills are the techniques and tools that make building your way to your goal easier and more effective

Good luck with your exams!

Introducing mindfulness

The mindfulness practices in this book can help you to stay calm and focused as you revise for your exams.

Important

If you feel that stress and anxiety are getting on top of you, speak to an adult that you trust. Opening up about how you feel can really help in dealing with what can be an intense time.

If you have recently experienced the loss of a loved one, a traumatic event or have been diagnosed with a mental illness, or have any ongoing physical pain, it's really important that you check in with someone (such as a parent, teacher, counsellor or doctor) before doing these practices.

What is mindfulness?

Mindfulness is a great way to help you prepare for exams. But what is it and how does it work?

Mindfulness is essentially awareness. It is about training your attention to notice your thoughts, feelings, sensations, and anything around you that is happening right now, without judging them. By doing this, you step away from automatic responses and observe what it means to be in the present with an open mind. This can help you to make better, more skilful decisions.

Your brain can be 'rewired' to work in more helpful or skilful ways. In many ways it's like brain training. Just as people go to the gym and lift weights regularly to build muscle, so mindfulness helps train the brain by doing the practices daily.

Preparing for exams

Neuroscientists are just starting to understand more about how mindfulness practice can help. Studies indicate that it helps in two main ways, especially when it comes to exams.

1 It helps to increase the density in the front of your brain. This is the part of the brain associated with memory, your ability to solve problems and to manage distraction.

2 It helps us to manage strong or difficult emotions. Feeling some stress and anxiety around exams is natural and, indeed, can help boost performance. It's when this becomes too much that it becomes a problem.

Mindfulness helps to calm activity in the bit of your brain associated with worry.

Connecting mind, body, emotions and behaviour

Mindfulness isn't just about training the mind – it's also about you connecting with your emotions and your behaviour.

Emotions and feelings can affect our bodies and our actions, and vice versa. Just as thinking can affect physical reactions (for example, feeling anxious can cause 'butterflies' in the tummy before an exam), so your body can affect your thinking.

By becoming aware of emotions, you can try to deal with them before they grow too strong or start to take over your thinking. Some of the practices in this book will help you reconnect with your body.

Doing and being

Very often, it is easy to want to get straight into doing a task like revision just to get it finished and out of the way. This is called **doing mode** – it helps you to gets things done, but not always to consider the **best way** of tackling the task.

Mindfulness helps by giving you a moment to pause and enter **being mode**. This allows time for you to ground yourself and be fully focused on the present moment, so you experience things more fully. Usually this will help you to take a calmer and wiser approach to a task, which will mean you're more effective. The practices that you are given in this book can help you to create this mental space.

Moving into being mode

The pressures of revision and exams may make you feel that taking 'time out' from revision to do these practices is not possible. However, regularly doing even short practices, where you can drop into 'being mode', can begin to give you greater mental space or clarity.

You can practise the following simple exercise to help you come out of doing mode and move into being mode, which creates a more mindful, moment-by-moment experience. It might seem a bit silly to start off with, when you're so used to doing a task without giving it much thought. However, the purpose of doing this exercise is to move away from doing things automatically and, instead, start to be fully in each moment and experience it more completely through all the senses.

Mindfully making a drink

- What can you hear? For example, notice the sound of pouring the drink or boiling water.
- What can you smell? For example, for tea or coffee, notice how the smells change as you make the drink.
- What can you see? For example, notice the colours and how they change.
- What can you feel? For example, the warmth or coolness of a drink in your hands.
- What can you taste? For example, if taking a sip of drink, notice how it first tastes and any changes in taste.
- Enjoy being in the moment as you consume your drink.

When you take time to slow down and live in a more moment-to-moment way, you are able to experience life more fully and appreciatively.

This can then help to create a greater sense of calm.

This simple exercise can have a big impact. Many people find they notice and taste far more.

Practising mindfulness

In addition to everyday mindfulness, you can do more formal practice, which is sometimes referred to as **meditation**. Just like learning any new skill, for example playing a sport or an instrument, mindfulness is something that has to be practised daily to have richer benefits. Doing daily practices of ten minutes or so can really help you to move your awareness to be fully in the present moment in a non-judgemental way, helping you to avoid overthinking, which can lead to worry, anxiety and stress.

Practices in this guide

This guide includes three introductory practices which are useful techniques to help ground and anchor you in the present moment and encourage you to be accepting and kind to yourself. The practices are:

- Mindfulness of Breath and Body
- The Body Scan
- The Three-Step Breathing Space

Each practice is accompanied by an audio file.

If you are interested in mindfulness, speak to your teacher to see if a course is running in your school that can give you a structured programme to follow, or search online for "mindfulness in schools".

Being kind to yourself

Exam preparation can be a stressful time, so it's important to take some time out regularly to be kind to yourself: to recharge your batteries, give your brain some breathing space, and acknowledge all the good preparatory work you're putting in. Take regular breaks and enjoy some 'downtime' with your friends and family to help recharge. Using the three practices regularly will help keep you calm and focused during your revision period.

Good posture for practice

Getting your posture correct for doing mindfulness practice is really important. The practices in this guide can be carried out in a seated position, or lying down.

Try to find a chair you can sit in that allows your feet to rest fully on the ground with your ankles, knees and hips all at right angles, with your back slightly away from the back of the chair so you can sit upright in an alert, but not tense, manner. Being comfortable will help to reduce distraction – but don't choose a chair that's so comfy that you fall asleep!

The room you choose should be somewhere you won't be disturbed. Turn your phone onto silent or flight mode. Let the people you live with know that you'll be doing mindfulness practice so that they do not disturb you.

Mindfulness can help you take a healthy, effective approach to your revision. But remember, you will still need to plan and revise!

Mindfulness practices

 **Practice 1: Mindfulness of Breath and Body**

Very often our minds like to wander. In this practice, you focus your attention on your breathing and on different parts of your body. It's a bit like shining a torchlight so that you focus on just one thing at a time, feeling the sensations that arise. Practising this regularly helps the mind wander less, which leads to less worrying and helps with concentration. Remember – it is normal for your mind to wander while you are meditating as that is what minds do! You are just trying to train it.

If your mind wanders, try to bring it back with a sense of kindness. It doesn't matter how many times the mind wanders, it's bringing it back each time to the focus on the breath or the body that's important, as you are increasing your concentration and training your attention each time. Don't be frustrated, as it is just part of training your brain.

The **Mindfulness of Breath and Body** practice will help you to develop your awareness and focus, which can help with revision. In addition, focusing on breath also has a calming effect (great if you are worrying about exams). Moving the focus to the body can also help to identify physical feelings caused by stress. Examples of stress in the body might be 'butterflies' or cramps in your tummy, your hands shaking, getting sweaty, or your mouth going dry.

Use the QR code to access the audio file for the practice.

To access the audio file for Practice 1, please scan the QR code or visit http://activetea.ch/32wQnxo

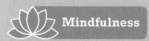 **Practice 2: The Body Scan**

Just as thoughts and emotions can affect our bodies, stress and tension in the body can affect our thinking and our feelings.

Constant analysis of problems (such as worrying about exams) can be exhausting and doesn't really help to find a solution. Sensing what's going on in your body can help to reduce the amount of time you spend analysing your problems. It grounds you back into your body, allowing you to see where you might be holding emotions and feelings as stress / tension in different parts of the body.

In the **Body Scan** practice, you move attention to different areas of the body, which allows you to feel where you might be holding emotions, such as worry. As you hold each different part of your body in awareness, really explore what feelings or sensations are arising in each one. This can help you to move away from thinking or analysing your problems too much. It can also improve posture, which, in turn, can improve thinking.

Use the QR code to access the audio file for the practice.

To access the audio file for Practice 2, please scan the QR code or visit http://activetea.ch/306mG4R

95

Mindfulness practices

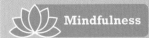 **Mindfulness**   ## Practice 3: The Three-Step Breathing Space

Worrying about what has gone on in the past or what might happen in the future cannot change events, and distracts you from the present – from what you are doing now. The present is something that you can change, so that is where your focus should be. For example, worrying about your exams in several months' time won't be as helpful as revising now! Don't let your future worries get in the way of actually achieving what you want now – to keep on track with exam preparation!

The **Three-Step Breathing Space** practice helps you to fully ground yourself in the present, to check in with how you are in that moment, and gives you a few moments to rest and recharge. The practice is structured a bit like an hourglass.

1 Firstly, you do a 'weather check' of the mind, to see what's going on, by observing your thoughts, giving you a more objective viewpoint of how busy or calm your mind is.

2 Then you turn your attention to your breath, helping to focus you in the present moment.

3 Finally, you expand out that awareness to sensations in the rest of your body, becoming aware of where you may be holding any emotions in the body as stress or tension.

The Three-Step Breathing Space is a very useful practice if ever you start to feel stressed and want a pause to help you step back and get perspective. The really great thing about this practice is that you can do it in three minutes or less. You can also do it anywhere. Think of it as your 'pocket practice', which you can use to 'recharge' yourself while revising or ground yourself just before or even during your exam.

Use the QR code to access the audio file for the practice.

To access the audio file for Practice 3, please scan the QR code or visit http://activetea.ch/34EAMh4

Progress tracker

Complete the challenges in each chapter of this book, and record your triumphs on this progress tracker. When you reach green for each of the topics, you will have developed great study skills!

	Challenge 1	Challenge 2	Challenge 3
Chapter 1: Motivation	☐	☐	☐
Chapter 2: Organisation	☐	☐	☐
Chapter 3: Time management	☐	☐	☐
Chapter 4: Learning to learn	☐	☐	☐
Chapter 5: Speaking and listening	☐	☐	☐
Chapter 6: Finding answers	☐	☐	☐
Chapter 7: Writing	☐	☐	☐
Chapter 8: Remembering	☐	☐	☐
Chapter 9: Revising	☐	☐	☐

Just started

Nearly there

Nailed it!

Glossary

Abbreviation [44]: A shortened form of a word or phrase. An abbreviation that is made up of the initial letters of other words and which is pronounced as a word is called an acronym – e.g. SCUBA.

Academic honesty [56]: Not using other people's words or ideas without acknowledging where these have come from.

Accelerate [33]: Make something go faster.

Acknowledging [56]: Recognising that someone else has done something you like.

Analysing [38]: Breaking a concept up into the parts that make it up so you can understand how it works.

Anticipate [14]: Expect, predict.

Audit [76]: An inspection of something that has got a particular purpose or goal.

Auditory learning style [79]: Using your listening skills to help you learn.

Authentic [56]: Real, genuine.

Brainstorming [36]: Writing down everything you can think of about a topic or connected to it in any way at all.

Candidates [60]: People (students) who are doing an exam are called exam candidates.

Command terms [60, 66]: The words in an exam question that tell you what to do to answer the question, e.g. 'describe', 'compare', 'explain'.

Commitments [29]: Things you have to do for other people.

Compiling [35]: Putting together.

Concept map [1]: A diagram that shows how different topics or points are related to each other.

Condense [84]: Make something more concentrated.

Context [63]: The wider setting of something that helps you understand that something better.

Counterproductive [16]: Something that gives you the opposite result from what you wanted.

Course glossary [63]: A list of the specialist terms for a course you are taking.

CV (curriculum vitae) [3]: An overview of your achievements and interests.

Deadline [21]: The end point to a process when you need to have achieved something specific.

Deciphering [17]: Working out what something means, step by tricky step.

Deep learning [4]: Becoming fully engaged in your learning.

Definition [63]: An explanation of what a word means.

Enhancements [55]: Improvements.

Essay [64]: A piece of writing on a specific topic or that answers a specific question.

Evaluate [2]: Decide what is good and what is not so good about something.

Extended writing [60, 64]: When you need to write quite a lot to explain what you think about something, taking care to structure your writing so that what you are saying is clear and easy to follow.

Flashcards [85]: A card with something to remember or learn on one side, and the answer or more information on the back.

Flow diagram [86]: A diagram that shows the sequence of steps that happen in a process.

Focused listing [36]: Listing the things you can remember about a topic.

GAPS [60]: When you are writing, think about Genre, Audience, Purpose, Style – GAPS.

Genre [60]: A specific style of art, music, literature; a category.

Glossary [63]: A list of key terms and their definitions.

Goals [11]: A result that you want to achieve.

Hit list [63]: Originally a list of people who needed to be killed! Now it means a list of very urgent tasks.

Ideas funnel [36]: A strategy for selecting the best ideas or points from a big list of ideas or points.

Index cards [84]: Small cards used for recording information: great for revision notes.

Infographics [35]: Information that is presented in a visual way.

Journey technique [73]: A memory technique that pegs things you need to remember onto a mental journey.

KWL [34]: Know, Want to know, Learned – a learning strategy.

Learning approaches [35, 39]: Different approaches to learning – most people use a mix of them in different ways and at different times.

Learning to learn [3]: Experts have shown that if you think about how you learn and what you find helps you learn best, then you will improve your learning.

Limitations [20]: Restrictions, things that mean you can go so far but no further.

Mark scheme [87]: A document that explains to examiners how they should mark answers to a particular exam question paper.

Memorise [69]: To learn something 'by heart' so you can remember it later.

Mindfulness [43]: A relaxation technique that helps you focus on where you are and what you are doing.

Mnemonics [4, 70]: Techniques to help you remember things.

Motivation [2]: What makes you do something.

Non-negotiable [29]: An agreement about something that you can't get out of or go back on.

Number pairs [72]: A memory technique that helps you remember a list of things by making unusual links to numbers.

Object [62]: The part of a sentence that shows the thing that something is being done to.

Objectives [12]: Steps on the way to achieving a goal.

Over-commitment [29]: When you have more commitments than you can handle in the time available.

Past papers [78]: Exam papers for your subjects from previous years.

Perspectives [46]: Viewpoints or points of view, for example 'she's got an interesting perspective on that problem'.

Pitfall [48]: A potential problem; a common mistake that people make in a particular situation.

Plagiarism [56]: Pretending that other people's work or ideas are your own work or ideas.

Planner [15]: A diary-style book which allows you to enter important school work like homework, deadlines, exams and revision, in order to plan and organise them alongside your other interests and everyday tasks.

Prioritise [15]: Put something ahead of something else because it is more important in some way.

Process [21]: A series of steps or operations or actions that change something into something else.

Procrastination [8]: Using distractions to avoid doing something.

Productively [30]: In a way that produces good results.

Read / write approaches [35]: Learning by reading and writing.

Recall [10]: Remember.

Reflection [5]: Looking back on your learning and thinking about what you did and how well it worked.

Relevant [7, 88]: Relating directly to something; meaningfully connected to a topic.

Reporter's questions [45]: Questions for investigating a topic thoroughly: who?, what?, when?, where? why? and how?

Research [51]: A way of investigating something in a step-by-step, systematic process.

Resources [21]: Materials, products, assets – things you use to achieve something or make something.

Review [26]: Look back over a process and decide what was good about it and what could have gone better.

Revision [78]: To look back over something so you can remember it.

Reward [9]: Something you get in return for having done something (or tried to do it).

Schedule [17]: A plan that identifies what needs to be done by when.

Six Thinking Hats [47]: A thinking strategy for group discussions which uses different kinds of roles to encourage different perspectives on a problem.

SPaG [60]: Stands for Spelling, Punctuation and Grammar – extra marks in exam questions for good written English.

Specialist terms [60]: Key terms that are used when a subject needs to be very specific and exact about a topic or concept.

Specification [63]: A document from an exam board that sets out what you need to learn for a GCSE subject.

SQ3R [4, 51]: An active reading technique: SQ3R stands for Survey, Questions and 3Rs: Read, Recall, Review.

Strategic learning [4]: Having a plan or goal for your learning.

Study dojo [6]: A special place for studying, or even a state of mind you can use to get yourself ready for effective studying.

Subject [62]: The part of a sentence that shows the thing that is doing something.

Superficial [63]: Just on the surface, not very serious or meaningful.

Surface learning [4]: Learning the basic knowledge required for further study.

SWOT [38]: A tool for evaluating ideas: looking at Strengths, Weaknesses, Opportunities and Threats.

Thinking skills [36, 39]: The skills that help you think about things differently, creatively, effectively.

Time bank [80]: The total amount of revision time you have between now and your last exam.

Time targets [18]: Giving yourself mini deadlines to help get through a task in good time.

'To do' list [18]: A list of things that you need to get done.

Verb [62]: The part of a sentence that shows what is being done.

Visual cues [35]: Linking a mental image with key information to help you remember.

Visual approaches [35]: Learning by seeing things, picturing them.

Weird pairs [4, 71]: A memory technique that makes connections between items on a list by linking them in weird ways.

It's true! References

It's true!

7 Murayama, Pekrun, Lichtenfeld, vom Hofe: Predicting long-term growth in students' mathematics achievement, *Child Development*, 2012

9 Bruno, Fiorillo: Why without pay? Intrinsic motivation in the unpaid labour supply. *The Journal of Socio-Economics*, 2012

15 Abikoff, Gallagher, Rosenblatt: Research findings on the Organizational Skills Training Program, 2011

20 Allen: *Getting Things Done*, 2002

24 Britton, Tesser: Effects of time-management practices on college grades. *Journal of Educational Psychology*, 1991. Macan, Shahani, Dipboye and Phillips: College students' time management: Correlations with academic performance and stress. *Journal of Educational Psychology*, 1990

30 Interview with Gloria Mark, Too many interruptions at work? *Gallup Business Journal*, 2006

33 Higgins, Wall, Falzon, Hall, Leat: *Learning to Learn in Schools Phase 3 Evaluation*, 2006

34 Higgins: Learning to Learn, *Beyond Current Horizons*, 2009

39 Sebba, Deakin Crick, Yu, Lawson, Harlen: A *Systematic Review of Research Evidence of the Impact on Students in Secondary Schools of Self and Peer Assessment*, 2008

42 Adler, Rosenfeld, Proctor: *Interplay: the Process of Interpersonal Communicating*, 2001

43 Carney, Cuddy, Yap: Power posing: Brief nonverbal displays affect neuroendocrine levels and risk tolerance. *Psychological Science Online*, 2010

44 Gilstrap, Martin: *Current Strategies for Teachers: A Resource for Personalizing Instruction*, 1975

51 Nachmias, Gilad: Needle in a hyperstack: Searching for information on the world wide web. *Journal of Research on Technology in Education*, 2002

53 Nachmias, Gilad: Needle in a hyperstack: Searching for information on the world wide web. *Journal of Research on Technology in Education*, 2002

69 Willis: *Research-Based Strategies to Ignite Student Learning*, 2006

70 Levin, Glasman, Nordwall: Mnemonic vocabulary instruction: Additional effectiveness evidence. *Contemporary Educational Psychology*, 1992

71 Miller: The magical number seven, plus or minus two: Some limits on our capacity for processing information. *Psychological Review*, 1956

85 Dunlosky, Rawson, Marsh, Nathan, Willingham: *Improving Students' Learning with Effective Learning Techniques: Promising Directions from Cognitive and Educational Psychology*, 2013

Answers

Now try this page 7

1 Page 8
2 Pages 13 and 14

Now try this page 10

1 Search Engine = research skills; Empath = listening skills; Words of Power = communication skills, how you present information; Mighty Mind = problem-solving skills, effective learning; Master / Mistress of Time = time management skills; Cook Up a Storm = effective learning techniques; Summoner = revision and memory skills.

Now try this page 12

1 Shelly

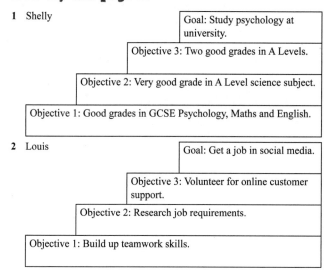

Goal: Study psychology at university.

Objective 3: Two good grades in A Levels.

Objective 2: Very good grade in A Level science subject.

Objective 1: Good grades in GCSE Psychology, Maths and English.

2 Louis

Goal: Get a job in social media.

Objective 3: Volunteer for online customer support.

Objective 2: Research job requirements.

Objective 1: Build up teamwork skills.

Quick quiz page 13

1 Page 10
2 Amelia Earhart

Now try this page 15

1 Page 16
2 Page 21

Quick quiz page 22

1 Page 18
2 Your brain hates to leave things unfinished.

Now try this page 24

1 Pages 27 and 28
2 Pages 29 and 30

Quick quiz page 31

1 This answer will be individual to you. Pages 27 and 28 show you how to work it out.
2 Page 29.

Now try this page 33

1 Pages 36, 37 and 38
2 Five minutes

Quick quiz page 40

1 Strengths, Weaknesses, Opportunities, Threats
2 Macbeth

Now try this page 41

Statements 1, 5, 6, 7 and 10 are all examples of learning to learn because they involve thinking about how you are learning and ways you could learn better.

Now try this page 42

1 Pages 43 and 44
2 Page 48

Quick quiz page 49

1 No
2 Six Thinking Hats

Now try this page 50

1 You can put whatever you like into the speech bubbles. Here's one suggestion in case you get stuck: Man – 'So, I've got something really important to tell you …', Woman – 'Oh no, I forgot to charge my phone!'
2 Remember to use body language; pay attention to what people say; improve concentration by using techniques like mindfulness; ask questions; give encouragement; try to avoid butting in; ignore distractions.

Now try this page 51

1 Read, Recall, Review
2 Pages 53 and 57

Now try this page 53

1 Something along the lines of: revision +"GCSE Maths" with a UK pages filter.
2 "sponge cake recipe" –eggs (or something similar)
3 Search for *Macbeth* in Google Books, and select Free Google eBooks from the Search tools / Any books menu.
4 Use the search option, e.g.: "world population increase" 1970–1990.

Quick quiz page 58

1 Survey, Questions, Read, Recall, Review
2 Page 53

Now try this page 59

These aren't really answers because the idea is you put the statements into your own words, but they tell you a bit more about the statements.
1 This is from *Romeo and Juliet* by William Shakespeare. It means that what is important is what something is, not what it is called.
2 This is about evolution: the idea that life started on Earth as one very simple organism, which then evolved into different organisms, which then evolved and evolved over billions of years to produce everything currently alive on Earth.
3 This is a quote that is often attributed to Winston Churchill about how difficult it is to stop people getting the wrong idea about something, especially if the truth is less exciting and more complex.

Now try this page 60

1 Page 62
2 Page 66

Quick quiz page 67

1 Spelling, Punctuation and Grammar
2 The advantages of dog ownership are that they provide companionship through their affection and loyalty as well as the health benefits associated with exercising them.

Now try this page 68

1 = f; 2 = a; 3 = e; 4 = c; 5 = d; 6 = g; 7 = b.

Now try this page 69

1 Pages 71, 72 and 73
2 Page 75

Quick quiz page 76

1 Page 71
2 Page 71

Now try this page 78

1 Page 79
2 Page 89

Quick quiz page 90

1 Assonance is when vowel sounds are repeated.
2 Edward VIII (see page 77)

Published by Pearson Education Limited, 80 Strand, London, WC2R 0RL.

www.pearsonschoolsandfecolleges.co.uk

Text and original illustrations © Pearson Education Limited 2014
Produced and typeset by QBS Learning Ltd
Cover illustration by Eoin Coveney

The rights of Rob Bircher and Ashley Lodge to be identified as authors of this work has been asserted by them in accordance with the Copyright, Designs and Patents Act 1988.

First published 2014. This edition 2020

23 22 21 20
10 9 8 7 6 5 4 3 2 1

British Library Cataloguing in Publication Data
A catalogue record for this book is available from the British Library

ISBN 978 1 292 31887 5

Printed in Italy by L.E.G.O SpA

Text credits

14: © Estate of Arthur Ashe, © Anne Frank Foundation, 1986; 46: The Nine Belbin Team Roles by Dr Meredith Belbin, © 2019, BELBIN Associates.

Photograph acknowledgements

(Key: t-top; b-bottom; c-centre; l-left; r-right)

Alamy Stock Photo: keith morris 2, Westend61 GmbH 20b(b), ONOKY – Photononstop 29r, RubberBall 32r, moodboard 52, Jan Miks 62, TongRo Image Stock 70t, Cultura Creative (RF)/79cl, Juice Images 88b; **Datacraft Co., Ltd:** 32,54; **Getty Images:** arekmalang 6,77, Comstock Images 2,7cr, Stockbyte 11, damircudic/E+ 16b, anton petukhov/Moment Open 17, Bombaert/iStock 20b(c), Zoonar 26, seb_ra/iStock 29l, Tim Macpherson/Cultura 32,46, Pixland 32,46, JGI/Jamie Grill 63, Michael Burrell/iStock 69l, Geir Pettersen/DigitalVision 69cr, Jasmin Merdan/Moment 69r, Thinkstock Images/Stockbyte 79tl, Caiaimage/Chris Ryan/ OJO+ 79tr, Caiaimage/Sam Edwards 79bl, Westend61 88t; **Glow Images:** Image 100/Corbis 78; **Imagesource:** Powerstock 16cl; **MIXA Co., Ltd:** 21; **Pearson Education Ltd:** Jörg Carstensen 2,24tl,24br, Studio 8 24tr, Jules Selmes 24bl, MindStudio 43, Jon Barlow 50, Naki Kouyioumtzis 70b; **Shutterstock:** 7tr, 79br, Kdonmuang 71, Sergei M. Kharitonov 16cr, Antonov Roman 20tr, Carlos Amarillo 20b(a), LightField Studios 27, antoniodiaz 42l, Antonio Guillem 42r, wrangler 67, Phovoir 69cl, Eiko Tsuchiya 70c, HBRH 79cr, Jojje 84t, Syda Productions 84c, Eiko Tsuchiya 84b, AndreyCherkasov 93

Note from the publisher

Pearson has robust editorial processes, including answer and fact checks, to ensure the accuracy of the content in this publication, and every effort is made to ensure this publication is free of errors. We are, however, only human, and occasionally errors do occur. Pearson is not liable for any misunderstandings that arise as a result of errors in this publication, but it is our priority to ensure that the content is accurate. If you spot an error, please do contact us at resourcescorrections@pearson.com so we can make sure it is corrected.